INSIGHT COMPACT GUIDES

TU**S**

CW00373652

GREAT LITTLE GUIDES

Compact Guide: Tuscany is the ultimate quick-reference guide to this extraordinarily varied region of Italy. It tells you everything you need to know about Tuscany's attractions, from the Renaissance wonders of Florence to the Leaning Tower of Pisa, the rugged coastlines of Livorno to the lush hills of Chianti, and the cool climes of Carrara to the broad plains of the Maremma.

This is one of almost 100 titles in *Insight Guides'* series of pocket-sized, easy-to-use guidebooks intended for the independent-minded traveller. *Compact Guides* are in essence travel encyclopedias in miniature, designed to be comprehensive yet portable, as well as up-to-date and authoritative.

Star Attractions

An instant reference to some of Tuscany's most popular tourist attractions to help you on your way.

Pisa, p25

Siena, p32

Florence, p16

Lucca, p37

Arezzo, p41

Prato, p48

Montecatini Terme, p51

San Miniato, p55

Castiglioncello, p64

Massa Marittima, p66

Chianti country, p69

Tuscany

Introduction

Places

Culture

Leisure

Practical Information

Tuscany – a gentle and noble region

Opposite: San Miniato

Tuscany – the name immediately conjures up images of *Chianti* and Michelangelo, Renaissance architecture and cypress trees. It's the sheer wealth of different impressions – from the beauty of works of art to the delights of the seaside – that give this region of Italy its very special and abundant charm.

The unparalleled artistic achievements in Tuscany began with the works of the Etruscans, a happy, enthusiastic race, merry with wine, and true lovers of life. Their heritage is perhaps reflected in the fact that Tuscany became the greatest centre of Renaissance culture and humanism. Indeed, Tuscany can even be said to have given birth to the Renaissance; in his paintings, Giotto projected Tuscany into space. Brunelleschi crowned space with his Florentine dome, the greatest feat of Renaissance engineering.

Raphael's Maddalena Doni

The result of 2,500 years packed with history are visible at every turn, and all this marvellous culture is rightly combined with a long tradition of pure enjoyment and celebration. The evening stroll, or *passeggiata*, across the piazza is as much a part of it all as the simple ingredients that make up the delicious Tuscan food. Today's wealthier Florentines also like to enjoy the luxury of combining the bustle of the city with the peace and quiet of a country estate, just as the Medici family used to do many centuries ago.

This close connection between town and country has always been a distinctive feature of Tuscany. A trip to Florence without an excursion to the hilly Chianti wine country, a stay in Siena without seeing the desert-like regions of dried clay known as *crete*, or a visit to Pisa without the smell of the sea air – it's impossible to imagine one without the other.

For centuries artists and writers have come to the region and found inspiration. The unique cultural monuments here gain a special energy from the idyllic natural landscape surrounding them, and it's this harmony between nature and art that so enchants visitors.

An Italian saying describes Tuscany as *gentile* (gentle) and *nobile* (noble). The whole region exudes benignity, with its picturesque undulating hills, its beautiful coastline and its delightful inhabitants. And the works of art in the cities and towns have an nobility and grandeur all their own.

Anyone who drives along the curving country roads past olive groves and vineyards and through the odd small village will probably come closest to the charms of Tuscany: a Romanesque church or a medieval palazzo will suddenly surprise, and the small bar on the piazza is just the place to sit back and simply soak it all in.

5

Getting around town

Tranquil olive groves

Position and Size

Tuscany (*Toscana*) is a region of central Italy on the Tyrrhenian Sea made up of the provinces of Arezzo, Firenze, Grosseto, Livorno, Lucca, Massa Carrara, Pisa, Pistoia, Prato (since 1993) and Siena. It covers a land area of 22,992sq km (8,876sq miles); the coastline is 572km (355 miles) long. Tuscany is bordered in the northeast by the Apennines and the Apuan Alps; the lowlands to the south are either inland valleys such as that of the Arno, or coastal plains like the Maremma. The highest mountains are Monte Prato (2,053m/6,735ft) in the north and Monte Amiata (1,738m/5,702ft) in the south. Tuscany's largest cities are Florence (pop. 392,800), Livorno (pop. 165,500), Prato (pop. 166,000) and Pisa (pop. 97,000).

Landscape

The particular attraction of the Tuscan landscape is its variety. In the north, rough Alpine peaks up to 2,000m (6,561ft) in height lie right next to the sandy beaches of the Tyrrhenian Sea. The Apennines with their chestnut forests contrast vividly with the hazy, undulating landscape between Florence and Siena, and the rocky bays along the Etruscan Riviera give way almost imperceptibly to the former swamp region of the Maremma with its sandy beaches and pine groves.

Livorno's old port

The flora reflects the various types of soil and differences in altitude; there are palm trees and mountain forests, hills covered with *macchia*, the almost desert-like *crete* (see page 70) south of Siena, shady pines along the beaches and gnarled conifers high up on steep mountain slopes. All of them exist within just a few kilometres of each other.

Stretching out on the sand

The scenery regarded as typically Tuscan is characterised by soft ridges lined by rows of dark-green cypresses, gold and yellow fields of grain, and olive trees shimmering almost white in the soft sunshine – nearly half of Tuscany really does look like this.

The fields and valleys of Tuscany, where nature has been tamed and formed by the hand of man for centuries, resemble one vast area of parkland, and constitute one of the most beautiful and environmentally appealing regions in Europe. The isolated farms, the villas and even the smaller towns all blend in perfectly with the all-pervading sense in Tuscany of everything being at ease with itself and at one with nature. The various different shades of yellow, green and ochre gain a special intensity when bathed in the magical southern light, and this is reflected in the luminosity of many of the works of art inspired by the landscape.

An inspirational landscape

When to Go

In winter the temperature can often be as high as 15°C (60°F), the museums and churches are almost devoid of tourists, and the staff in hotels and restaurants have time on their hands and are far more relaxed and friendly.

In summer, however, temperatures can reach 40°C (104°F) and hordes of tourists arrive from all over the world. Tuscany, and especially cities and towns like Florence, Siena or San Gimignano, are totally overrun. By way of contrast, the beaches are less crowded with visitors than those up on the Adriatic, for instance. Most of the people holidaying on the Tuscan coast in the summer are locals fleeing the heat of Florence or Siena.

Elbow to elbow in Siena

Population

The last Italian census (1991) recorded a Tuscan population of just over 3.5 million, roughly 1.42 percent less than the previous decade. The number would have been a lot lower without all the immigrants to the region, for Italy has the lowest birth rate in the world – Tuscany being no exception. The drop in population in the provincial towns was particularly drastic at almost 6 percent. Italians are leaving the big cities and moving into the suburbs or out into the countryside. The population is at its densest in the Arno Valley, and at its lowest in the centre and the south of the region.

Siesta smiles

7

Political Life

The Tuscan population has always voted left. During the last regional elections in 1990 the Communist Party (PCI), still in existence at that time, won 39.9 percent of the vote and the Socialists 13.6 percent; during the national elections in 1994 the new progressive left-wing coalition won all the direct mandates to both chambers.

Tuscany is one of the 15 new regions that were set up in 1970 (Italy has 20 regions altogether), but it is far from being federalist. Tuscany's constitution resembles those of the other 14 regions created at the same time in that it leaves hardly any room for the region to make its own decisions, pass its own laws or make any private income of its own. Even though Tuscany has a regional parliament, a president and a council of ministers, it is still almost exclusively controlled by Rome.

Tuscany is divided into 10 provinces: Arezzo, Firenze, Grosseto, Livorno, Lucca, Massa Carrara, Pisa, Pistoia, Prato (since 1993) and Siena. The provinces are governed by a state-appointed prefect who is far more powerful than the provincial parliament.

Local municipalities have hardly any power of decision. They have no direct income, and their activities as a whole are supervised by a state-appointed secretary.

Religion

Although over two-thirds (74 percent) of Tuscan couples choose a church wedding, religion now plays less of a role in many people's lives, and most congregations have been reduced to a handful of old women. Religious traditions, such as processions or festivals in honour of patron saints, are nevertheless still celebrated by everyone, and remain very popular.

Tuscans adore a good celebration, and statistics show that they're also very keen to be entertained: the outlay on music, theatre and the cinema here is the third highest in all of the 19 Italian regions.

Campanilismo

Ask someone from Maidstone where he comes from and he'll probably say 'Kent'. But if you ask someone from Lucca the same question he won't answer 'Tuscany' – he'll say 'Lucca!' This reaction reflects Tuscany's historical division into lots of small self-governing city-states. Tuscans have never developed any kind of regional pride, and have always considered the grand duchy of Tuscany to be something artificial. Even today, pangs of jealousy are felt when, say, Florence wants to extend its airport, even though Pisa's Galileo Galilei Airport is more practically situated. The Italian word for this fierce local pride is *campanilismo* – literally, 'church-tower politics'.

Mezzadria farms are a common feature

Mezzadria

Mezzadria, or the practice of renting a farm for half the produce, is widespread in Tuscany, and accounts for the isolated farmhouses that are such a typical feature of the landscape. The city-dwellers who owned most of the land allowed the farmers to use it in return for half (*mezza*) the harvest. Each farmer was also given a farmstead as

The Campanile in Siena

8

close as possible to his fields, and these houses, known as *poderi*, can still be seen all over the place.

Sagre – Festivals of Self-Indulgence

Sagre are festivals based around one product, eg *sagra della fragola* (strawberries), *del tortello* (stuffed pasta), *del cinghiale* (wild boar), *del fungho* (mushrooms), etc. Tuscany has an inordinate number of different *sagre* for all manner of delicious products, and eating fine food and drinking with friends is one of the region's favourite occupations.

The Tuscan Dialect

Tuscans are justifiably proud of their dialect, which was raised to the highest literary level by Italy's greatest authors and poets: Dante, Petrarch and Boccaccio all wrote in Tuscan (Florentine) dialect, and in the 16th century it became the official national language. Today it is regarded in very much the same way as Oxford English.

la Bottega del naturista
Prodotti altamente selezionati

PIENZA Corso Rossellino 16 Tel.0578/748081

Food to nourish body and soul

Economy

Tuscany's most well-known exports are its superb wines, such as *Chianti*, *Brunello* or *Vino Nobile*, and its excellent olive oil. But the economy is by no means predominantly agrarian. Only 61,000 people – 4.5 percent of the region's population – work in the agricultural sector, while a full third of all Tuscans are employed in industry in the Arno Valley, and over 60 percent in the service sector. The latter is a growth industry, and almost 8 million tourists annually (3.6 million of them from abroad) provide a guaranteed income for many people.

Industry in Tuscany, as elsewhere, is in recession. In the last decade alone almost 100,000 jobs have been lost. The only way most of the smaller companies have kept their heads above water is by concentrating on high-quality products; elegant shoes, textiles, leather goods and stationery of fine design remain popular exports.

High quality is definitely the hallmark of local wines. Fifteen percent of the land reserved for Italy's excellent DOCG wines lies in Tuscany. Olive oil production received a major setback in the winter of 1985/6, when many of the gnarled old trees in the region failed to survive the extraordinary cold. The farmers had to start all over again, and while they are now beginning to plant more trees and reinvest in the industry, this is changing the landscape: many of the ancient trees standing haphazardly about the fields have been replaced by sensible-looking straight lines of saplings.

Should *contadini* (farmers) ever find themselves having to sell, at least in this part of Italy they can rest assured that they will get a good price from foreign buyers.

Historical Highlights

Around 900BC Villanovan (Early Iron Age) settlements appear in the region occupied by today's Tuscany.

800–500BC Etruscan civilisation flourishes. Dodecapolis, a confederation of 12 states, includes Arezzo, Cortona, Chiusi, Fiesole, Populonia, Roselle, Vetulonia and Volterra.

280BC The Romans conquer the last of the Etruscan cities.

59BC Caesar founds Florence.

AD200–600 Tuscany is occupied by a succession of migrating tribes, including the Visigoths, Ostrogoths, Byzantines and, finally, the Lombards.

AD570 Lucca becomes the capital of the Lombard duchy of Tuscany.

774 Charlemagne conquers the kingdom of Lombardy. Tuscany is now subject to the German emperor.

1000–1300 German emperors conquer Italy; constant warring between Guelfs (supporters of the papacy) and Ghibellines (supporters of the Holy Roman Empire).

11th century Pisa becomes a sea-power in the Mediterranean.

12th–14th century After the death of Matilda of Tuscany in 1115, the cities of Tuscany gradually affirm their independence. Prosperous burghers demand to elect their own town governments in a bid to reduce imperial power. Amost all the towns in Tuscany win the right to elect their own government.

In the 13th century the craftsmen and merchants (*popolo*) elect their own council headed by the *capitano del popolo*. Tuscans spread across Europe from the Mediterranean to the north, working as bankers and merchants.

1289 Serfdom abolished.

1348 Plague kills a third of the population of Florence.

1384 Arezzo is conquered by Florence.

1406 Florence conquers Pisa, thus creating a regional state in Tuscany.

1434 Cosimo de Medici comes to power in Florence.

15th century Florence becomes the most important centre of culture in Europe. The Renaissance reaches its peak under Cosimo de Medici, and his grandson Lorenzo the Magnificent.

1530 Emperor Charles V gives Tuscany to the Medici as a duchy.

1555 Cosimo I de Medici successfully persuades Siena to join the duchy.

1569 Pope Paul V promotes Cosimo to the rank of grand duke of Tuscany.

17th century The duchy experiences a steady decline in its fortunes.

1737 Death of the last of the Medicis, Gian Gastone; Tuscany now becomes the property of Duke Francis of Lorraine, husband of the empress Maria Theresa of Austria.

1737 Napoleon's first Italian campaign.

1799–1815 Napoleonic interlude.

1808 Annexation of Tuscany by the French Empire.

1815 The Grand Duchy is absorbed into the Austro-Hungarian Monarchy.

1847 The Free Republic of Lucca is integrated into the duchy.

1848 War of Independance.

1859–60 After several uprisings by the local population, the Austrians are forced to leave Tuscany. In a referendum the Tuscans vote to join the Kingdom of Piedmont-Sardinia.

1861 Proclamation of the Kingdom of Italy.

1865 Florence becomes the capital of the new kingdom.

1871 After the occupation of Rome, Florence loses its function as capital. Tuscany shares the fate of the Italian Union.

1915 Italy enters World War I on the side of the Allies.

1922 Benito Mussolini comes to power.

1940 Italy forms a pact with Germany and Japan and enters into World War II.

1943 Fall of the Fascists. Mussolini executed at the end of the war, in 1945.

1944 The Gothic Line, the defensive wall of the German troops in the Apennines, extends along the northern border of Tuscany, turning it into a battleground.

1946 Italy becomes a republic.

1957 Treaty of Rome: Italy is a founder member of the EEC (now the EU).

1966 The Arno bursts its banks; flooding in Florence destroys irreplacable works of art and many valuable collections.

1970 Fifteen new regions are formed, Tuscany included. The first regional elections are won by the Communists.

1985 A great frost destroys over half of Tuscany's olive trees.

1987 A terrorist bomb in Florence kills five and damages the Uffizi.

1993 Prato becomes the 10th province.

1994 Italy exchanges Proportional Representation for a first-past-the-post system. In the parliamentary elections, all the direct mandates to the senate and house of representatives in Tuscany go to the left-wing progressive coalition.

1996 In the parliamentary elections, all but one of Tuscany's representatives are members of the centre-left alliance.

Famous Tuscans

The three most famous Italian writers were all born in Tuscany: Dante Alighieri (Florence, 1265–1321), Francesco Petrarch (Arezzo, 1304–74) and Giovanni Boccaccio (Certaldo, 1313–75

The greatest architects and artists in Italy also came from Tuscany: Leonardo da Vinci (Vinci, 1452–1519), Giotto (Vespignano, 1267–1337), Vasari (Arezzo, 1511–74), Masaccio (Florence, 1401–28), Donatello (Florence, 1386–1466), Brunelleschi (Florence, 1377–1446) and Michelangelo (Caprese, 1475–1564).

Galileo Galilei (Pisa, 1564–1642) was one of the most important astronomers and physicists of all time; his research freed science from the dust of the Middle Ages and gave it a sound empirical basis.

Giacomo Puccini (Lucca, 1858–1924) and Pietro Mascagni (Livorno, 1864–1945) are two of Italy's most famous composers.

Machiavelli

The Italian statesman and writer Niccolò Machiavelli (1469–1527) has gone down in history as the father of modern political science. His work *Il Principe* (*The Prince*), which he wrote in 1513, was a handbook for rulers; its main theme is that they must always be ready to do evil if they believe that good will come of it in the end. The Roman Catholic Church naturally condemned this work out of hand, but could do nothing to stop it being published.

The author's work was closely associated with his own experiences: Machiavelli began his career by studying the classics, and from 1498 onwards he worked under the newly re-established Florentine Republic. As head of the Second Chancery he went on a number of diplomatic missions to France, Switzerland, Germany and also to the pope.

His close ties with the Republic and its leading families meant that he swiftly fell into disfavour with the Medici on their return in 1512: he was imprisoned and tortured for a year. He hoped that he would be able to win back the respect of the rulers with *The Prince*, but had no success at first. He retired to his country estate in Sant'Andrea near Florence and devoted himself to studying political history, writing a series of discourses on Livy, a treatise called *The Art of War*, and *Mandragola*, a comedy about a seduction. He died in 1527.

Florence Cathedral
Preceding pages:
Typical Tuscany

Route 1

Florence

Florence (pop. 387,500), the capital of Tuscany, is one of the three most important cultural cities in Italy alongside Venice and Rome. All the famous Renaissance artists, not just Michelangelo, created unique masterpieces here; Florence has an unbelievable number of churches, palaces and museums. Even a month is insufficient time to see everything that Florence has to offer.

The city offers the art and culture of the past combined with the elegance and friendliness of contemporary Florentines. It's only in high summer that the masses of tourists get in the way of the sights. At this time of year the Duomo and the Piazza are best left to them; the less well-known areas of the city such as San Lorenzo or San Frediano provide the opportunity to discover everyday life in an Italian city which in many ways retains all the charms of a small town.

History

Florence was founded by Julius Caesar, who chose the site on the banks of the Arno for a colony of veterans in 59BC. All that remains today of this original Roman settlement is the rectangular street-plan and the former forum (today's Piazza della Repubblica), easily recognisable on any city map. In early medieval times Florence was overshadowed by several more prosperous towns on the *Via Francigena* (the old road across the Apennines from Emilia into Tuscany), and it was only in around the year 1000 that the city began to increase in importance. Goods traffic was shifted to the Via Cassia – and this turned out to be very favourable for the Florentine economy.

The first architectural masterpieces began to appear, such as the baptistery and the church of San Miniato al Monte. The city's wealth increased further thanks to its wool and silk processing industry and its banking activities. Soon Florentine merchants and bankers were travelling all over Europe.

In Florence itself the merchants joined forces with the craftsmen to form guilds (*artes*) and took over the government of their free commune, which, by the end of the 13th century, had a population of 100,000 and was one of the largest cities in Europe. It was at this stage that monumental structures started appearing all over Florence as they had done earlier in Pisa and Lucca. Foundation stones were laid for the Bargello, the Palazzo Vecchio and the great churches of the mendicant orders. Influential Florentine families such as the Pitti and the Strozzi competed with the Medici not only for political but also architectural supremacy. This rivalry often resulted in violence, but came to an end in 1434 with the return from exile of Cosimo de Medici, who took over as de facto ruler (*signore*) of Florence.

Florentine bankers

The Florentine aristocracy was looking for models on which to base its new republican state from the end of the 14th century onwards. The virtues and values of ancient Rome became fashionable, and people began admiring and studying the art, philosophy, literature and languages of antiquity. Man was once again at the centre of the universe, and the long period of cultural darkness between the downfall of the Greek and Roman classical world and its rediscovery was now defined as the 'Middle Ages' by the new scholars of the Renaissance.

Lorenzo de Medici

The antique conception of beauty now dominated the arts; faithful copies of Roman and Greek statues were in great demand, and the fabulous creations of Romanesque art and Gothic forms from medieval times were forgotten about. Members of rich Florentine families, most notably Lorenzo de Medici, became the generous patrons of artists, architects and philosophers. Rivalry between the various leading families was often expressed through the various magnificent sculptures, paintings and buildings they regularly commissioned.

It was the Florentine republic's subjugation of the city-states surrounding it, from Fiesole all the way to Pisa, which altered its basic character. Tuscany was bequeathed to the Medici as a hereditary duchy by Emperor Charles V in 1530. Florence lost its autonomous status and was incorporated into the new duchy. It was only between 1865 and 1871 that the city had another – albeit brief – moment of glory when it became the capital of Italy and the place of royal residence.

The view from Piazzale Michelangelo

Sights

The city centre is closed to private cars but all the sights can easily be reached either on foot or by bus: a day ticket (*biglietto turistico*) costs L5,000 and can be used on any of the orange buses in Florence and Fiesole (ATAF line).

San Miniato al Monte interior

There is a breathtaking view of Florence from the ★ **Piazzale Michelangelo ❶**. The vast sea of houses below stretch across to the gentle hills surrounding the city; the Arno is a silvery strip of light, spanned by innumerable bridges, and the Ponte Vecchio attracts the eye almost magically. Above everything is the gloriously red cupola of the Duomo.

A little further on is another view of Florence every bit as good, from the square in front of one of the city's oldest churches, ★★ **San Miniato al Monte ❷**. After the baptistery, this ancient church is the most important Romanesque structure in the city. The magnificent mosaics on its facade and inside exercise a special fascination, intensified still further by the Gregorian chants sung by the monks during evening prayers in the crypt.

The best place to begin a tour of the city proper is the Piazza del Duomo, with its grandiose combination of cathedral, campanile and baptistery.

The ★★★ **Baptistery ❸** is one of the most perfectly-formed buildings in the whole city. Even Dante, like many of his contemporaries, thought it dated from antiquity. It was actually built during the 11th century, and its special expressiveness lies in the harmonious synthesis of the marble decoration and the architecture.

Baptistery door detail

The gilt bronze ★★ **portals** of the baptistery are masterpieces and have been admired for centuries. The oldest one, the southern portal, was created in 1330 by Andrea Pisano and shows 20 scenes from the life of St John the

Baptist, Florence's patron saint. The north portal, illustrating the life of Christ, the four evangelists and the four fathers of the church, is by Lorenzo Ghiberti (1387–1455), who also executed the elegant *Door of Paradise* opposite the Duomo with 10 reliefs depicting scenes from the Old Testament. Inside the baptistery are some magnificent mosaics, created in around 1270 by skilled Venetian artisans.

The church of Santa Reparata used to stand opposite the baptistery. The site has been built over several times since antiquity, and Roman mosaic flooring as well as remains of an old 4th-century church can still be seen today beneath the ★★ **Duomo di Santa Maria del Fiore ❹**. The Florentines began building a cathedral on the site in 1296, feeling that the little church of Santa Reparata was not representative enough in view of their city's new-found importance. Florence wanted to outdo its rivals, Siena and

Duomo di Santa Maria del Fiore

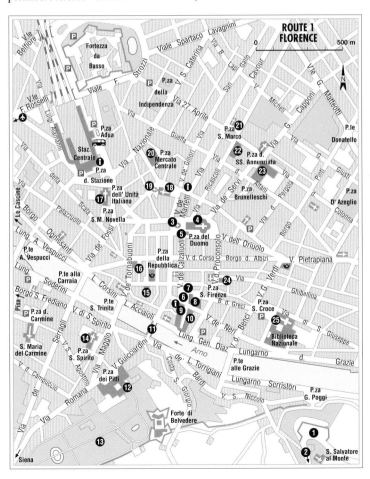

Brunelleschi's cupola

The Campanile

Neptune Fountain, Piazza della Signoria

Pisa, and one of the largest churches in the world was duly constructed, 153m (501ft) long and 38m (124ft) wide. The architect who received the commission, Arnolfo di Cambio, was told to build 'the most beautiful church possible'. There were ambitious plans for the cupola, too; in 1418 Filippo Brunelleschi won the commission to build it. No-one really believed that the vault would be self-supporting during construction, or that his idea of having two concentric shells would ever be realised – but in 1436 Brunelleschi's 107-m (351-ft) high cupola was completed.

The three-aisled interior is quite simple after all the colour outside. Nevertheless, the windows, the fine majolica reliefs above the sacristy doors and the paintings in the vault of the cupola (restored in 1994) all provide more than enough magnificence. There is a famous painting of Dante in the left transept; in 1465 a public reading of his *Divine Comedy* took place here at the request of the Florentine Republic. From the top of the ★★ **Campanile** (bell-tower) ❺ there is a view of the sea of red roofs in the city centre, and all the palaces and churches. The campanile was built by the cathedral master architect Giotto, who spent far more time on it than on the Duomo itself. He began the bell-tower in 1334, and the three-colour marble decoration was his idea; his successors extended the campanile to its final height of 84m (275ft). The hexagonal bas-reliefs – the originals are in Tuscany's finest cathedral museum, the **Museo dell'Opera del Duomo** (Monday to Saturday 9am–6.50pm, shorter in winter) behind the cathedral – are typically Renaissance. They portray man at the centre of everything: human history begins with the creation of Adam; his initial progress is depicted via the *artes minores* (crafts); the seven planets can be seen influencing his destiny; then he achieves perfection via the seven virtues, the seven liberal arts and the seven sacraments.

The Via dei Calzaiuoli, one of the city's most important shopping streets, connects spiritual Florence with its secular counterpart. Restaurants here charge exactly twice the amount for *panini* consumed while seated, although only a few steps away down the side-streets it's an entirely different world: small bakeries, fruit and cheese shops, wine stores and *trattorie* all vie for the customer's attention. For a cappuccino or a chocolate in more elegant surroundings, there is the chic Caffè Rivoire in the atmospheric **Piazza della Signoria** ❻.

Cosimo I had this piazza decorated by his favourite artists: his equestrian statue is by Giambologna (1594), and the **Neptune Fountain** by Ammannati (1575); together with Vasari they gave 16th-century Florence the new face that Cosimo wanted. Next to the baroque fountain is a stone marking the spot where the monk Savonarola was executed in 1498.

On the left-hand side of the piazza is the **Alberto della Ragione Collection** ❼ (weekdays except Tuesday 9am–2pm, Sunday 8am–1pm), with its 20th-century works by De Chirico, Carrà, Morandi and Guttuso.

The massive fortress-like building dominating the square is the ★ **Palazzo Vecchio** ❽ (weekdays except Thursday 9am–7pm, Sunday 8am–1pm). It was originally built by Arnolfo di Cambio for the *Priori*, the presidents of the city's guilds who ran the city (hence its other name, the Palazzo della Signoria). The building was based on a similar one in Volterra, although this one is massive in comparison and seems to be carved out of a single block. The battlements and the tower round off the palazzo's majestic simplicity.

Palazzo Vecchio

The magnificent interior courtyard, redesigned in Early Renaissance style in 1453 by Michelozzo, already hints at the stunning beauty of the state rooms inside the building, especially the breathtaking ★ **Hall of the Five Hundred**. Cosimo I had this former assembly hall for the government of the republic turned into a magnificent chamber. The paintings on the walls and ceiling are by Vasari and his workshop. Sculptures by Michelangelo, Giambologna and Verrocchio adorn the many other rooms.

19

It was the Swiss mercenaries (*Landsknechte*), once stationed in a guardroom here, who gave the arcaded ★★ **Loggia dei Lanzi** ❾ its name. It was built between 1376 and 1382 as a ceremonial grandstand for the city fathers, and contains Giambologna's last and most famous work, *The Rape of the Sabines* (1583). The three-figure group, which is a wonderful example of the Mannerist principle of sculpture, has lost none of its original power. Right next to it stands Benvenuto Cellini's impressive bronze masterpiece *Perseus* (1545), brandishing the head of the Gorgon Medusa.

Rape of the Sabines

Interior courtyard, Loggio dei Lanzia

Ponte Vecchio

Primavera by Botticelli

After the conquest of Siena in 1555, the Medici needed an administrative centre to supervise their duchy, which then encompassed almost the whole of Tuscany. This is why Vasari designed the ★★★ **Uffizi** ❿ (Monday to Friday 8.30am–6.50pm, Sunday and public holidays 8.30am–1.50pm) for Cosimo I; the word means 'offices'. The 45 rooms inside this building today contain what is probably the world's most important collection of paintings. Alongside a comprehensive collection of Tuscan art (from Cimabue and Giotto to Botticelli, Leonardo da Vinci and Michelangelo) the museum also owns several magnificent works from other parts of Italy (Raphael, Titian, Tintoretto, Caravaggio), many German (Dürer, Cranach, Holbein) and also Dutch (Rubens, Rembrandt) masterpieces.

The view of the Arno from the windows of the Uffizi also includes the oldest and most picturesque bridge in Florence, the ★★ **Ponte Vecchio** ⓫. It was built in 1345, and looks splendid at any time of day, though particularly so when the evening sun is reflected in the water. It 'sparkles' in another sense too: at the end of the 16th century Grand Duke Ferdinand I reserved the exclusive use of its shops for gold- and silversmiths.

A little further along the opposite bank of the Arno, the massive ★★ **Palazzo Pitti** ⓬ (Tuesday to Saturday 8.30am–6.50pm, Sunday 8.30am–1.50pm) comes into view on the left-hand side. It was built in around 1440 by Brunelleschi for the Pitti family, who were rivals of the Medici. In 1549 the Medici had become so powerful that they forced the Pitti to sell the palazzo. Ammannati, one of Cosimo's favourite architects, extended the building to make it the largest in Florence; the facade is 205m (672ft) long and 38m (124ft) high. Cosimo thus turned an average palazzo into a regal residence. The eight museums within – ranging from the state rooms (*appartamenti monumentali*) to the famous ★★ **Galleria Palatina** – certainly

Empire chair, Galleria Palatina

cater for all tastes; there's even a silver museum. Behind the palazzo is the magnificent baroque park known as the **Giardino di Boboli** , the perfect place to wind down after sightseeing. Beyond the grotto by Buontalenti, the amphitheatre and the **Neptune Fountain** stands a charming little coffee-house where Austrian archdukes once enjoyed the spectacular view of Florence.

Statue of Abundance, Boboli Gardens

The Piazza Santo Spirito is named after the Renaissance church of **Santo Spirito** , built by Brunelleschi, and situated a few streets further away. This lively area of Florence is called **San Frediano**, and has preserved its original character with its *trattorie*, small shops and craft workshops (especially furniture restorers). The Via Maggio and Via di Santo Spirito contain several antiques shops. In the summertime the local signoras place their chairs outside their front doors for a chat with the neighbours. Snacks are available in the bar on the piazza; the Tuscan specialities in the old-fashioned 'Cantinone del Gallo Nero' at Via di San Spirito 6R are a lot more substantial.

An idea of how noble families used to live in their palazzi can be gleaned from a visit to the fascinating **Palazzo Davanzati**  (Tuesday to Sunday 9am–2pm); the rooms here give a unique opportunity to experience medieval interior furnishings at first-hand.

21

Close by are even more palazzi, but these ones have window displays and contain some of the most exquisite fashion items in the city. The **Via de Tornabuoni** is Florence's most elegant shopping street, and is home to names like Gucci and Enrico Coveri.

The massive **Palazzo Strozzi** , formerly the property of the Strozzi family, is impossible to miss, but the grand 'Giacosa' bar on the opposite side of the street is certainly worth looking for.

From the palazzo, several charming little streets lead to the broad Piazza Santa Maria Novella, where the magnificent Renaissance facade of the church of ★★**Santa Maria Novella**  suddenly comes into view. Many of the city's wealthy families – the Strozzi, the Rucellai, the Gondi, the Tornabuoni and several others – commissioned the decoration for the chapels in this church. This was partly a way of salving their consciences at earning such vast quantities from their investments, and partly a very good way of rising in each other's esteem. The marvellous frescoes in the main choir chapel were commissioned from Domenico Ghirlandaio by Giovanni Tornabuoni, who thus gave his family a lasting monument. Giovanni and his wife can be seen praying at each side of the window, and the young woman in the gold brocade dress is their daughter, Ludovica. This very realistic fresco gives a good impression of the fashion of that time.

Santa Maria Novella, with fresco detail

There's a 15th-century masterpiece in the left-hand side-aisle that should not be missed on any account: the ★ **Fresco of The Trinity** by Masaccio (1427). Instead of being set against a blue or golden heaven, God is seen here framed by Renaissance architecture – only in Florence could this have been done. The painting doesn't seem all that special at first glance, but it revolutionised the use of perspective in Renaissance art.

The church of ★★ **San Lorenzo** ⓲ looks unfinished – the grandiose marble facade designed by Michelangelo was never actually built. Brunelleschi altered it to suit the tastes of the Medici, and a look inside at the harmonious and magnificent Renaissance interior is definitely worthwhile; the two pulpits by Donatello are also very fine.

The **Cappella Medici** ⓳ (Tuesday to Saturday 8.30am–1.50pm) can be reached from the other side of the church. The 'Cappella dei Principi' is opulent, but the ★★ **New Sacristy**, begun by Michelangelo, is a real masterpiece; it contains the Medici tombs and combines classical elegance, power and sublimity. Leo X, the Medici pope, wanted this family mausoleum (1520) to display all the glory of his family. The two rather insignificant dukes of Nemours and Urbino (the son and the uncle of Lorenzo the Magnificent) were given the most important tombs of the Renaissance by Michelangelo – it's an irony of fate that Lorenzo himself and his brother Giuliano had to content themselves with the *Madonna and Child* statue. The muscular *Day* and the young woman asleep representing *Night* lie on the tomb of Giuliano of Nemours; opposite, the powerful *Dawn* seems to be awaking from sleep on the tomb of Lorenzo, and *Dusk* is going to sleep – a sculpture group of an expressiveness unequalled at that time. That Michelangelo was confident that his art would

Ceiling of the Cappela Medici

22

Central Market Hall, fresh produce guaranteed

endure is clear from his response to contemporary critics who told him that Giuliano's face was not true to nature: 'In one thousand years, no-one will notice.'

The central **Market Hall** ⑳ is an interesting iron construction dating from the 19th century. The selection of boars' heads and unplucked poultry here is picturesque and the produce guaranteed fresh. Tourists and locals tend to mix here in the San Lorenzo area – housewives coming from the market, students (the university is around the corner), or businessmen meeting after work in the bars.

The magnificent baroque church of **San Marco** ㉑ (Tuesday to Saturday 8.30am–1.50pm) is situated nearby. The ★★ **museum** to the right houses Fra Angelico's blissful frescos. Entranced by its magical charm, many people linger awestruck in front of his ★★ **Annunciation.** Great elegance is on display in the ★ **Accademia** ㉒, the art academy where Michelangelo's famous *David* can be found and also his sculpture group *Prigioni* ('The Prisoners'). Though incomplete, they are among the artist's most impressive works (Tuesday to Saturday 8.30am–6.50pm, Sunday 8.30am–1.50pm).

The famous David

The **Spedale degli Innocenti** ㉓, or Foundling Hospital, with its graceful colonnade of nine arches, was designed in 1419 by Brunelleschi; the charming terracotta roundels between the arcades are by Andrea della Robbia. This building pays tribute to the humanist ideals and social commitment of the Florentine Republic; it was financed by the silk guild *(arte della seta)*.

Terracotta roundel

23

One of the finest buildings in the city is the 13th-century fortress known as the ★★ **Bargello** ㉔ (Tuesday to Saturday 8.30am–1.50pm) in Via del Proconsolo; it contains one of the most important collections of sculpture in the world. It was built between 1255–61 as the city's first town hall. Although it pales in comparison with the Palazzo Vecchio, the Bargello's richly-decorated halls provide the perfect backdrop for the fine sculpture on display.

'Vivoli', in the Via Isola delle Stinche (near the broad Piazza Santa Croce) is renowned for the best ice cream in Florence. On the piazza is another very famous Florentine church, ★★★ **Santa Croce** ㉕. This Franciscan building has over 270 sepulchral slabs set into its pavement, and its walls are lined with the tombs of Italy's great and famous men: Michelangelo, Dante, Rossini, Galileo and Machiavelli.

Aspects of Santa Croce

As with the other mendicant order churches in the city, wealthy families such as the Bardi or the Peruzzi (first and second chapels to the right of the main altar) commissioned the decoration of the individual chapels in Santa Croce. Giotto painted the two extraordinary fresco cycles depicting scenes from the life of St Francis of Assisi, St John the Baptist and St John the Evangelist. It was in around

1330 that Giotto reached the summit of his genius, and his colourful and detailed compositions represent a final farewell to the rigidity of Byzantine art.

The magnificent sacristy leads to a section of the monastery which today houses the Florence leather academy; good quality items are sold here at reasonable prices. The area around the Piazza Santa Croce contains several shops specialising in leather goods.

Children in Florence will enjoy the Science Museum, Piazza dei Giudici 1 (Monday to Friday 9.30am–1pm) and also the Archaeological Museum (Tuesday to Friday 9am–2pm, Sunday 9am–1pm) with its fascinating finds from the Etruscan era.

Excursion to ★★ Fiesole

Fiesole is 8km (5 miles) northeast of Florence (journey time: ½ hour). Take the No 7 bus, leaving from the Duomo and stopping at Piazza Mino da Fiesole in the town centre.

Florence from Fiesole

The small and much older town of ★★ **Fiesole** (pop. 15,000) looks down on Florence from its hilltop. It was an important town in Etruscan times; under the Romans, as *Faesulae*, it became the capital of the surrounding region. During the Middle Ages Florence began to assert itself, until it finally conquered Fiesole in 1125.

Teatro Romano, Fiesole

On the central piazza are the characteristic **Palazzo Pretorio** and the Romanesque cathedral of **San Romolo**. The ★ **archaeological zone** (summer 9am–7pm, winter 9.30am–4.30pm), has a Roman theatre, thermal baths and temple, and walls dating from Etruscan times.

The church of **San Francesco** (summer daily 10am–noon and 3–6pm, winter until 5pm) offers a magnificent view and a museum containing a collection of Eastern *objets d'art* assembled by Franciscan missionaries.

The nave of San Francesco

Route 2

Pisa

Pisa cathedral and tower

Plenty of photo opportunities

Pisa (pop. 96,000) is world-famous for just one thing: the Leaning Tower. It towers above the magnificent Piazza del Duomo, which contains the city's most important sights: the Duomo, baptistery and Camposanto. It's sad that this one square is all that most tourists ever get to see of Pisa; they go home believing that Pisa consists of the Campo dei Miracoli and nothing else, and that it's constantly filled with masses of tourists clutching tasteless plastic towers purchased from souvenir salesmen.

History

For around 500 years the university and its professors and students have occupied a central position in Pisan city life. Before that the city's fortunes were determined by merchants and seafarers. The Romans used the mouth of the Arno as an base for their fleet, and during medieval times Pisa's economy was based entirely on sea-going trade. Victories over the Saracens and participation in the First Crusade with over 100 ships allowed Pisa to set up trading colonies right across the Mediterranean, and in the 11th century it was also one of the first independent communes.

The city's most important buildings date from this period, which lasted until the 13th century. Conflicts with its ambitious Guelf rivals, Genoa, Lucca and Florence, then ushered in Pisa's decline. In 1406, after a lengthy siege, the Florentines gained control of Pisa, and the maritime republic's days of glory were over. It was only from the 16th century onwards, after the foundation of its all-important university, that modern-day Pisa gradually developed. Pisa University today has almost 40,000 students.

Sights

The best place to begin a tour of Pisa is at the ★ **Piazza del Duomo ❶**, where the Leaning Tower, the Duomo and the baptistery soar above their green lawns. The white marble facing of all three structures emphasises the exquisite harmony of this piazza, which was realised not by any bishop or count but by the people of Pisa themselves, as an expression of their power and pride.

The ★★★ **Duomo ❷** (November to February Monday to Saturday 10am–12.45pm, Sunday 3–4.45pm; March and October Monday to Saturday 10am–5.40pm, Sunday 1–4.40pm; April to September Monday to Saturday 10am–7.40pm, Sunday 1–5.40pm) was one of the first monumental structures of the Middle Ages, built with the booty taken from the Saracens after the Pisan victory at Palermo in 1063. Buscheto, its architect, combined the ground-plan of an Early Christian basilica with a transept

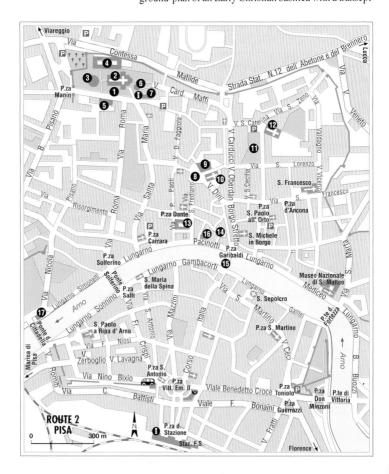

– the very first sacred building in the shape of a cross anywhere in Italy. Inside, the Duomo resembles an enormous mosque, mainly because of the generous use of arches in the aisles. Buscheto was familiar with Islamic architecture, and the ornate marble intarsia decoration on the outside of the building also reflects Islamic influence; many other features of the structure are typical of the Northern Italian Romanesque style. It is this mixture of styles that makes Pisa's cathedral architecturally unique.

The four-tiered arcaded facade of the building above three porches was completed under cathedral architect Rainaldo in the 12th century. This style, broken up by rhomboid and circular elements, occurs in several later sacred buildings in Western Tuscany (eg the Duomo and also San Michele in Foro in Lucca). This type of facade is thus referred to as 'Pisan-Lucchesan'.

Inside, the marble ★ **pulpit** by Giovanni Pisano (1302–22) is a masterpiece of Gothic sculpture. The work depicts Old Testament prophets and New Testament apostles.

Precisely aligned with the cathedral is the ★★★ **Baptistery** ❸ (daily in winter 9am–4.40pm, March and October 9am–5.40pm, April to September 8am–7.40pm). It was begun in 1153 by Diotosalvi in the same Romanesque style as the Duomo; the Gothic phase of its construction from the pillared loggia onwards was supervised by Nicola Pisano and later his son Giovanni (who designed the celebrated pulpit in the Duomo, *see above*). Lack of funds meant that the cupola could only be added in the 14th century. It was for the baptistery in 1260 that Nicola Pisano created the first ever free-standing ★ **pulpit**, one of the most important Late Romanesque works of art in Italy.

If one compares the bas-reliefs on this pulpit with the Roman sarcophagi in the **Camposanto** ❹ (daily in winter 9am–4.40pm, March and October 9am–5.40pm, April to September 8am–7.40pm), the monumental cemetery on

Nave of the Duomo and the facade

27

Interior of the Baptistry

The famous tower

Statue, Museo del Duomo

the northern side of the piazza, it becomes clear where Nicola Pisano gained his inspiration. These magnificent sarcophagi were used as tombs during the Middle Ages. Before its destruction in 1944 the cemetery was decorated by the largest expanse of medieval frescoes in the world. The sections that still survive, including *The Triumph of Death* and *The Last Judgement*, may now be visited.

The fascinating **Sinopia Museum ❺** (daily in winter 9am–12.40pm, 3–4.40pm; March and October 9am–5.40pm; April to September until 7.40pm) on the south side of the piazza reveals several earlier versions of the frescoes. A *sinopia* is the term used to describe the sketch for a fresco that was made in red earth pigment on the rough wall before the plaster was added; these earlier drawings were discovered during the restoration work.

The ★★★ **Campanile ❻**, or Leaning Tower *(Torre Pendente)*, is one of the best-known structures in the world. Bonnano began work on it in 1173. The tower already began to lean during its construction and thus became immediately famous. In the year 1275, after a lengthy interval, Giovanni di Simone, the architect of the Camposanto and the Campanile of San Francesco, decided to continue with the tower and rectify the inclination as he went. Nevertheless, the structure continued to lean. To stop it collapsing, black boxes filled with lead were placed at the foot of the tower to act as a counterweight; not exactly aesthetic, but effective – since 1993 the inclination has receded slightly.

The highlight at the ★ **Museo del Duomo ❼** (daily in winter 9am–4.20pm, March and October 9am–5.20pm, April to September 8am–<u>7.20pm</u>) is the sculpture collection; there are several fine 12th-century works here, and also masterpieces by Nicola and Giovanni Pisano, Tino da Camaino and Nino Pisano. More magnificent works of sculpture can be admired in the ★ **Museo Nazionale di San Matteo** (Lungarno Mediceo) (Tuesday to Saturday 9am–7pm, Sunday 9am–1pm).

Students can be seen everywhere during Italian term-time (October to June) in the old part of the city; a favourite haunt is the ★ **Piazza dei Cavalieri ❽**, one of the most attractive squares in the city. This was the political centre of the Pisan Republic during medieval times until its importance was considerably diminished by Archduke Cosimo I – whose equestrian statue is everywhere in evidence. He founded the Order of St Stephen in 1561 to fight the Turks in the Mediterranean (in imitation of the Knights of Malta) and gave its members the **Palazzo della Carovana ❾**, the former council chambers of the Pisan Commune. The magnificent *sgraffito* decoration (floral patterns, coats-of-arms, symbols), restored in 1993, and

also the church of **Santo Stefano dei Cavalieri**  next door, were based on plans by Vasari; the church is usually only open in the morning. The interior contains several captured standards and sections of ships dating from Pisan naval victories against the Ottomans.

The trees and marble benches in the nearby **Piazza dei Martiri della Libertà** ⓫ provide some welcome shade and relaxation; lovers, students and old men all fight for room on these benches. Far less attention is paid to the imposing Pisan Gothic facade of the church of **Santa Caterina** ⓬, which was built between 1251 and 1300. It contains some particularly fine statues of the Annunciation by Nino Pisano.

The **University** ⓭ is just a few steps away from the Piazza dei Cavalieri. It is one of the oldest in Italy. Pisa had a *studio* as long ago as the 12th century, and it was given its first set of rules in 1329. After a failed attempt at reform under Lorenzo il Magnifico, who wanted to increase his control over Pisa via the university, the institution was sponsored anew by Cosimo I. Today it is one of the largest and most important universities in Italy, and attracts students from all over the country. The elite *Scuola Normale Superiore*, founded by Napoleon on the French model in 1810, has also contributed to Pisa's reputation as the intellectual centre of Italy. One in three Pisans has a university degree. The long tradition of scholarship here ranges from Leonardo Fibonacci, who spread the use of Hindu-Arabic numerals in the 13th century, and Galileo Galilei (1564–1642), Pisa's most famous son, to the physicist and Nobel Prize-winner Enrico Fermi (1901–54), who directed the first controlled nuclear chain reaction.

The medieval-style section of the city lies around the **Piazza delle Vettovaglie** ⓮, where there are several stands and small shops. The picturesque atmosphere is en-

The University is one of the oldest in Italy

29

Palazzo della Carovana

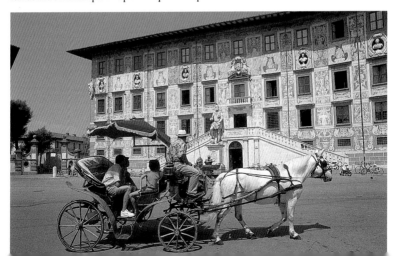

hanced still further by the attractive portico here, where the traders can be heard shouting their wares.

Borgo Stretto

In contrast to this busy market-place, the Borgo Stretto is a real oasis of tranquillity; it's an elegant shopping street with several quiet cafés in its arcades. The **Ponte di Mezzo** ⓯, first mentioned in 1109, is the bridge where the sham battle takes place on the last Sunday in June every year (*see Festivals & Folklore, page 82*). On the opposite side of the Arno is Pisa's main shopping street, the Corso Italia.

Pisa's only surviving brick palazzo, the **Palazzo Agostini** ⓰, is not only famous for its splendid 15th-century terracotta decoration; it also contains one of the city's most famous cafés, the 'Caffè dell'Ussero'. The pictures on the walls show some of the revolutionaries who assembled here during the *Risorgimento* (the liberation and unification of Italy in the 19th century).

At dusk, when the breeze blows from the sea, the sun sets behind the fortress-tower of the **Cittadella** ⓱, the red, yellow and ochre-coloured palazzi are reflected in the Arno, and the whole scene is framed by the dark mountains of the Monte Pisano, it's clear that Pisa is far more than just the Leaning Tower.

Romanesque Excursions from Pisa

There are several pretty little villages around Pisa with magnificent Romanesque churches dating from the 11th and 12th centuries. Ironically, it was lucky that Pisa's fortunes declined when they did, because all the churches that stood on Pisan-owned territory were never restored or altered since funds were unavailable.

The clock-tower in Cascina

Leave Pisa on the N67 in the direction of Florence, and then after San Casciano turn off towards the well-sign-posted *Pieve* (baptist church). The facade with its familiar Pisan arcatures, broken up by rhomboid and circular decoration, features some very fine reliefs by Beduino (c 1180); the animals are most realistically rendered. In **Cascina** (pop. 37,000), the town's covered arcades and **clock-tower** should be admired before a closer inspection of the typically Pisan facade of the 12th-century Pieve Santa Maria.

Vicopisano view

The medieval section of **Vicopisano** (pop. 7,700) is still marvellously intact; the seven towers give the whole place a very fortified appearance, strengthened still further by the fortress straddling the highest part of the hill. At the other end of the town is the impressive **Pieve SS Maria e Giovanni**, which was mentioned as early as the 10th century. The present structure clearly reflects the forms of Pisan Romanesque architecture. The three-aisled interior is rather severe and simple, but contains a surprising number of excellent works of art including an

11th-century *Deposition* carved in wood, which can be admired in the apse.

From Vicopisano either travel along the Arno, past the Pieve in Caprona (easily spotted from the road), and then on to Calci, or instead take the scenic, serpentine route across the mountains via Buti. One of the finest baptist churches in the area is situated in **Calci** (pop. 5,600); its three-aisled interior is divided by pillars with impressive capitals, almost all of them antique. The most striking work, however, is the **font**, created from a single block of marble by the Beduino workshop.

Roadside refreshments

Another excursion leads from Pisa to one of the most important Romanesque churches in Tuscany and also to the sea. Leave Pisa via the magnificent avenue of plane trees in the direction of Marina di Pisa and then turn off to ★ **San Piero a Grado**. Entering the basilica of , it takes a moment to adjust to the sheer magnificence of the architecture: the antique pillars and the fresco cycles. The sea once used to extend as far as here, and this is the spot where, according to legend, the apostle Peter (hence the name of the basilica) first set foot on Italian soil. The ★ **fresco cycle** in the nave, above the portraits of the popes, shows scenes from the life of St Peter.

The pleasant, old-fashioned bathing resort of **Marina di Pisa** is a fascinatingly decadent place. There's not much beach left, and swimming isn't recommended these days either because of pollution from the nearby Arno estuary. But a stroll along the beach promenade or a cappuccino in one of the many cafés can be quite enjoyable, and on a clear day the two offshore islands of Gorgona and Capraia can be made out in the distance.

31

Marina di Pisa beach

Siena rooftops

Route 3

Siena

Siena (pop. 55,500) and its *campo*, as the locals familiarly refer to the main square, the Piazza del Campo, belong together just like Pisa and its Leaning Tower. This shell-shaped square is the pride of the Sienese and it is where the city's heart beats fastest, especially during the *Palio*, the historic horse-race held here every year.

History

The Palio delle Contrade (*see Festivals & Folklore, page 82*) reminds the Sienese of their city's heyday when Siena was a free commune that governed itself, and its 17 *contrade*, or 'wards', played an important role in the life of the city. Siena owed its rise to prominence to its very

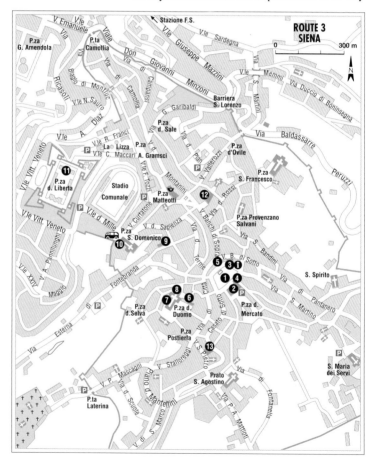

The distinctive fan shape of the Piazza del Campo

favourable location on the *Via Francigena* (the old road across the Apennines from Emilia into Tuscany).

Increasing economic prosperity meant that Siena's unique Gothic buildings could be built; they are still a distinctive feature of the city skyline today. The policy of expansion which led to the subjugation of the surrounding region finally brought Ghibelline Siena into conflict with Guelfian Florence. In 1260 the Sienese defeated Florence near Montaperti, but after a period of economic decline and the plague outbreak of 1348, Siena became increasingly insignificant. It flourished again briefly under the Piccolomini family during the Renaissance, but a long siege by the emperor Charles V in 1555 – financed by Duke Cosimo I – dealt the final blow to the city-state's independence.

33

Sights

Any tour of Siena has to begin at the ★★★ **Piazza del Campo ❶**. The harmony and unity of this square is instantly captivating. During the 13th century the Sienese government planned it just the way it looks today. The delightful fan-shape is emphasised by the white strips of travertine marble alternating with the red-brick herringbone paving. In 1297, to ensure that this harmony was retained, the commune issued strict regulations governing what could and could not be built in the piazza; not even private palazzi were exempted.

Palazzo Pubblico

The battlemented ★★ **Palazzo Pubblico ❷**, at the lowest part of the Campo, was built between 1297 and 1342, and rounds off the square nicely. Like almost all the palazzi in Siena, it has an upper storey of brick which is also a distinctive feature of the **Palazzo Sanssedoni ❸**, with its three storeys of Gothic windows.

The entrance to the 102-m (334-ft) high **Torre del Mangia ❹** (16 November to 14 March 10am–3.30pm, other-

Performing passeggiata

wise 10am–sunset), the proud symbol of the Sienese Republic, is inside the Palazzo Pubblico, which also contains the ★ **Museo Civico** (May to August 9am–7pm; April, September and October 9.30am–6pm; November to February and Sundays 9.30am–1.30pm). In this museum are exhibited the ★ *Maestà* (1315) by Simone Martini and also the first ever secular fresco cycle, ★ *Allegories of Good and Bad Government* by Ambrogio Lorenzetti, one of the few surviving forms of medieval political propaganda. It can be admired in the Sala della Pace, formerly the council chamber of the nine patricians who ruled the city.

Elegantly-dressed elderly ladies and gentlemen, affectedly casual young men and dolled-up young women are all very much in evidence at the **Croce di Travaglio** ❺, the intersection point of the three main shopping streets in Siena: the Via Banchi de Sopra, the Via Banchi de Sotto and the Via di Città. This is where the so-called *passeggiata* takes place every evening, when the Italians stroll up and down the street in order to see and – most importantly – be seen.

Statue in cathedral square

Duomo facade

These days the ★ **Duomo Nuovo** seems almost to have been a symptom of megalomania. It was begun in 1339, and the plan was to incorporate the present cathedral into it as a transept. This massive project was undertaken as a response to the Duomo in Florence, but had to be abandoned because of the disastrous effects of the plague outbreak of 1348. Today the three marble arcades and the facade and side portal of the Duomo Nuovo – all that was built of it – house what is perhaps the finest **Museo dell'Opera del Duomo** ❻ (daily November to mid-

March 9am–1.30pm, otherwise 9am–7.30pm, October 9am–6.30pm) in all Tuscany. It's worth a visit for the observation terrace alone, but also contains a true masterpiece: the *Maestà* (Madonna Enthroned, 1308–11) by the famous Sienese master Duccio di Buoninsegna.

The foundation-stone for Siena's Gothic ★★★ **Duomo** ❼ was laid at the end of the 12th century, but the building was only finally completed in the mid-14th century after the grandiose plans for the Duomo Nuovo had been abandoned. The facade, begun by Giovanni Pisano in 1284, is richly decorated with sculpture, and was the first in Italy to reflect the harmonious design of the great French Gothic structures.

Duomo: the inlaid marble floor

Even the pavement inside this cathedral, which is almost overfilled with works of art, merits closer inspection. The inlaid marble with its 56 'pictures', the result of two centuries of work by around 40 artists, was finally completed in the mid-16th century. The finest pictures are Matteo di Giovanni's pensive Sibyls and marble mosaics by Beccafumi. The octagonal marble ★ **pulpit** was created between 1266 and 1268 by Nicola Pisano and his workshop. It is a masterpiece of Italian Gothic sculpture, where the rigidity of design still evident in Pisano's Late Romanesque pulpit in the baptistery in Pisa (*see page 27*) has given way to fluid and dramatic movement.

The left-hand side-aisle leads to one of the finest Renaissance rooms in the world, the ★★ **Libreria Piccolomini**, which contains a magnificent fresco cycle by Pinturicchio. This stunning Renaissance library was financed by a nephew of Pius II, the Piccolomini pope, to house his father's collection of books (the same nephew later became Pius III, but lasted only 10 days). The splendid frescoes portray 10 scenes from the life of Pius II, with meticulous attention to detail. It was Pius II who commissioned the harmonious group of Renaissance buildings in his home town of Pienza (*see page 73*).

Between 1316 and 1325, when the Duomo Nuovo was still a going concern, the ★ **Baptistery of San Giovanni** ❽ was built beneath part of the cathedral. The entire structure is very imposing, but the Early Renaissance ★ **font** (1417–30) by Jacopo della Quercia definitely merits closer inspection; the scenes from the life of St John the Baptist on its sides were executed by several other leading artists of the day, including Donatello and Lorenzo Ghiberti.

The font in the Baptistery of San Giovanni

The **Santuario Cateriniano** ❾ (daily 9am–12.30pm, 3–5.30pm, summer from 2.30pm) is dedicated to St Catherine of Siena; in the summer, though, it's less of a sanctuary than a well-promoted tourist attraction. The Santuario grew up around the home of Caterina Benincasa (1347–80), whose eloquence persuaded Gregory XI to come back to Rome from Avignon. She was canonised in the 15th century by Pope Pius II before being proclaimed a patron saint of Italy in 1939. Her head lies in a reliquary in St Catherine's Chapel in the nearby church of **San Domenico ⑩**, which also contains some fine frescoes by Sodoma (1526).

The walls of the Medici fortress

From here it's a short walk to the **Forte di Santa Barbara ⑪** (daily noon–1am, Monday until 8pm, closed Sunday), built by Cosimo I after his defeat of Siena in 1560. The park here is delightful, and in the basement of the fortress is the *Enoteca Italiana*, where the best wines in Italy can be tasted and purchased.

The Piazza Salimbeni, with its imposing palazzi, is one of the most attractive squares in all Siena. The **Palazzo Salimbeni ⑫** at the centre became famous as the headquarters of the 'Monte dei Paschi', the oldest banking establishment in the world. It was founded in 1624.

Up beside the piazza there's another Sienese institution: 'Nannini'. The stuccoed bar owned by rock singer Gianna Nannini's father and racing driver Alessandro, plus the ice-cream outlet next door, form one of the most popular rendezvous points in the whole city.

Ice cream is always popular

Madonnas with enigmatic smiles are plentiful in the **Palazzo Buonsignori ⑬**, which houses the ★★ **Pinacoteca Nazionale** (Tuesday to Saturday 9am–7pm, Monday 8.30am–1.30pm, Sunday and public holidays 8am–1pm). This fine art gallery documents Sienese painting from the 12th to the 17th centuries, and includes works by Duccio di Buoninsegna, Ambrogio Lorenzetti and Sodoma. The early rooms are full of Madonnas, apple-cheeked, pale, remote or warmly human. The repetition of Siena's favourite theme focuses attention on style and colouring.

Two museums have recently opened near the cathedral: the **Museo Archeologico Nazionale** (daily 9am–2pm, Sunday and public holidays 9am–1pm, closed 2nd and 4th Sunday in the month) sheds light on Siena's earliest inhabitants, and the **Spedale Santa Maria della Scala** (November to March 10.30am–4.30pm, September and April, Saturday and Sunday 10.30am–5.30pm, summer until 6pm) provides a fascinating insight into the day-to-day life of a medieval pilgrims' hospice.

The countryside near Siena

Excursion to the ★ Abbey of San Galgano

The abbey of San Galgano was once the most powerful Cistercian house in all Tuscany, and today it stands in a remote beauty spot, surrounded by green fields. It was built between 1224 and 1288 in the French Gothic style, but had already begun to decay by the 16th century. Today the Gothic flying buttresses soar straight into the sky and the floor is overgrown with grass. The whole place has a deeply compelling stillness about it, very conducive to contemplation and meditation.

Route 4

Lucca from the Guigi Tower

Lucca

Lucca (pop. 86,000) is one of the most beautiful small towns in Tuscany, and has a special tranquillity that is irresistible. The town not only possesses many architectural and artistic masterpieces, it also has several excellent cafés, along with many shops where the service is friendly and the prices are more than reasonable.

37

History

The marshy plain on which Lucca stands, situated between the Apennines and Monte Pisano, was inhabited in Etruscan times. Little remains of the ancient Etruscan city of *Luk*, or of the Roman colony of *Luca*. Under the Lombards, Luca became the residence of a duke and the capital of *Tuscia* (Tuscany). The commune of Lucca was established at the end of the 11th century. Conflicts with Pisa and Florence endangered the little city-state on several occasions, but it managed to hold its own, and successfully governed itself until the Napoleonic era.

The increase in population that accompanied Lucca's prosperity meant that the original Roman town wall was no longer adequate, and a second one had to be built in around 1280. The town gates of San Gervasio and Protasio and the Portone dei Borghi still survive from this time. Lucca's most recent town wall was built between 1504 and 1645 by Flemish engineers, and was 4.2km (2½ miles) long. However, its 11 bastions, 30-m (98-ft) wide foundations and 12-m (39-ft) high brick facing were never once attacked. During the 19th century these fortifications were converted into today's park.

In 1847, Lucca became the last of Florence's rivals to be incorporated into the grand duchy of Tuscany.

The old fortifications are now a park

Facade of the Cathedral

Tomb of Ilaria del Carretto

Sights

This tour of Lucca starts at one of its finest buildings, the ★★ **Cathedral ❶**. The highly ornate Romanesque facade with all its pillars and decoration was the work of master architect Guidetto da Como (1204); the magnificent ★ **reliefs** on the portals illustrating scenes from the life of St Martin, and the reliefs depicting the 12 months of the year were also executed by Lombard sculptors. The *Adoration of the Magi* next to the left doorway has been attributed to Nicola Pisano.

The interior contains several fine works of art, the main attraction being Tintoretto's *Last Supper.* A highlight of (very) Early Renaissance sculpture can be admired in the north transept, the ★ **tomb of Ilaria del Carretto** (1405) by Jacopo della Quercia; the tender expression shown on the young woman's face is still Gothic, but the sarcophagus is definitely Renaissance.

The small tempietto in the left-hand side-aisle contains the famous wooden likeness of Christ known as the ★ *Volto Santo*. According to the legend, the artist was helped by angels. The crucifix crossed the Mediterranean miraculously and appeared on the beach in Luni; from there it was taken to the church of San Frediano in Lucca. To commemorate the transfer of the crucifix from San Frediano to the Duomo, a candlelight procession is held on 13 September every year. The golden, gem-studded 'clothing' the Volto Santo receives for this event can be admired in the town's newly-opened ★ **Cathedral Museum ❷** (daily 10am–6pm, winter weekdays mornings only; combined

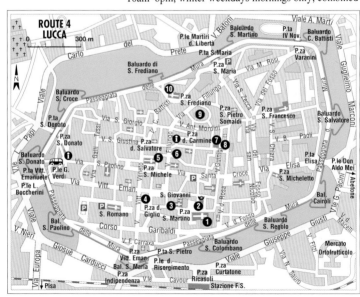

ticket with Santa Reparata), which also contains several very fine examples of medieval silversmiths' work.

A few steps away is the church of ★ **Santa Reparata** ❸ (same opening times as Cathedral Museum), formerly the most important sacred building in Lucca, with its Battisteria di San Giovanni. Santa Reparata contains one thousand years of architectural history: excavations beneath the church have revealed the thermal baths (2nd-century AD), the first Roman house on the site (1st-century AD), and sections of the Early Christian basilica (4th- to 5th-century) with its late 8th-century crypt. The building site for the 12th-century Romanesque church has, amazingly, been found preserved – complete with brick kiln and foundry – beneath the pavement in the nave. Roman mosaics, Lombard tombs and medieval inscriptions lend the place even more of a special fascination.

Excavations at Santa Reparata

Cross the broad **Piazza Napoleone** ❹ to the former Roman forum. The Pisan Romanesque church of ★ **San Michele in Foro** ❺ is definitely Lucca's pride and joy. Its 13th-century facade, with all its different columns and strips of marble, is most impressive.

39

Via Fillungo, Lucca's main artery, has a vast assortment of excellent shops (also down the side-streets). Well-preserved medieval buildings and the eye-catching 13th-century **clock-tower** ❻ compete for attention here with all the elegant shop-window displays. It's worth climbing the **Guinigi Tower** ❼ (November to February 10am–4.30pm, March to September 9am–7.30pm, October 10am–6pm) for a splendid view across the town and the hills beyond. This picturesque tower with the trees growing on its summit belongs to the 14th-century palazzo of the Guinigi family alongside it – and there's another **Palazzo Guinigi** ❽ just around the corner, bearing the family's colourful coat-of-arms.

Yet another building formerly owned by the family, the castellated Villa Guinigi (1418) (Tuesday to Sunday 9am–2pm), contains the **Museo Nazionale**, with many Etruscan and Roman finds, medieval sculpture and several paintings; the attractive brick villa also has a magnificent garden.

Statue at the Museo Nazionale

Back in the Via Fillungo, the artists' café 'Di Simo' at No 58 is definitely worth a quick visit; the composer Puccini, one of the town's most famous sons, used to be a regular here.

The **Piazza Anfiteatro** ❾ is the most spectacular square in Lucca. It follows the oval contour of the 2nd-century Roman amphitheatre on this site, and a few mighty sections of Roman masonry can still be seen at the northern edge of the square.

The large mosaic of the *Ascension* on the facade of

Piazza Anfiteatro

San Frediano

★★ **San Frediano ⑩** is impressive even from some distance away. The basilican three-aisled interior is magnificent, and just to the right of the entrance is a mid-12th-century ★ **font** richly carved with reliefs. It depicts scenes from the life of Moses (below) and the 12 apostles (above). St Zita, the patron saint of housewives, can be visited in the second side-chapel to the right; she died in the 12th century, and today her miraculously undecomposed body is a macabre sight. The best way to round off a visit to Lucca is with a stroll along its 16th-century ★ **ramparts**, which provide several excellent views of the town, its buildings, and the Apuan Alps.

Tuscan villas

Villas are as much a part of the Tuscan landscape as isolated farmhouses or rows of cypresses. Very close to Lucca there are several particularly impressive country houses that can be visited. Originally built as administrative centres for local agriculture, in which Lucca's merchants invested much of their money, many of these villas were extended from the 16th century onwards and converted into magnificent summer estates.

Leave Lucca on the N12 in the direction of Abetone, and after passing through Marlia, turn off to the **Villa Reale** (tours of the grounds daily March to November, Tuesday to Sunday 10am, 11am, 3pm, 4pm, 5pm and 6pm; July only Sunday, Tuesday and Thursday; December to February on request, tel: 0583-30 00 09). Large sections of the original baroque garden are still in existence. The open-air theatre here is one of the finest in Italy.

Villa Mansi

Continue now through a relatively built-up area to Segromigno, and on to the magnificent **Villa Mansi** (winter Tuesday to Sunday 10am–12.30pm and 3–5pm, summer10am–12.30pm and 3–6pm). Here the garden is less impressive than the actual villa, which is a baroque gem. The original rectangular building was given its eye-catching portico and double staircase in 1634. Inside, the Pompeiian-style grotesque paintings are particularly fine.

Garden of Villa Torrigiana

The **Villa Torrigiani** (March to November daily except Tuesday 10am–noon, 3–6pm; summer 10am–1pm, 3–7pm) is not far away. The drive there, along an impressive avenue of cypress trees, is an experience in itself; the villa with its magnificent facade is majestically situated on a slight rise at the end. There are some fine baroque rooms inside, and the grounds, too, are idyllic. In the right-hand part of the garden the water basin and the pretty *giardino segreto* ('secret garden') survive from baroque days; the grottoes, fountains and statues of *Hercules and the Four Winds* make this the most attractive villa in the Lucca region.

Route 5

Arezzo

Piazza Grande café

In 1992 Arezzo (pop. 92,000) celebrated the 500th anniversary of Piero della Francesca. Art-lovers from all over the world flocked to this picturesque town to admire his famous frescoes in the church of San Francesco. But to their great disappointment, restoration work had not been completed in time – and it was still going on in 1998.

History

Art in Arezzo has a long history. The town's great significance during Etruscan times continued after the Romans arrived in 294BC – the amphitheatre of the Roman town of *Arretium*, probably the largest in Tuscany, is ample evidence of this, and *vasi aretini*, red-clay pottery, was in demand all over the Roman Empire. Arezzo has had its famous sons, too: Maecenas, the patron of Virgil and Horace; Guido d'Arezzo (995–1050), inventor of the musical scale; Petrarch (1304–74) the poet, and the celebrated architect and art historian Giorgio Vasari (1512–74).

41

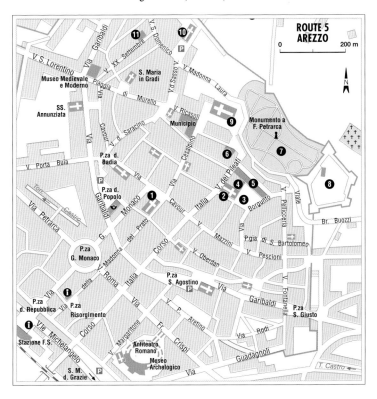

The free commune was weakened during medieval times by domestic squabbles and also by conflicts with Siena and Florence – so much so that Florence actually succeeded in purchasing Arezzo in 1384. Florentine influence was then omnipresent, and after a long period of decline Arezzo finally reestablished itself in the 20th century as a centre of trade and industry.

Sights

The Corso Italia, Arezzo's main shopping street, runs north to the political and religious centre of the town, and has been the most important thoroughfare since around 1200. Arezzo's main sight, the church of ★★ **San Francesco** ❶, is just a short walk away from the Corso. This 13th-century Franciscan structure is famous worldwide for the ★★★ **frescoes** by Piero della Francesca in its choir chapel (some parts undergoing restoration). Piero, born in San Sepolcro – his native town also has paintings by him – was one of the greatest Italian artists of his era, and his *Legend of the True Cross* is one of the most perfect fresco cycles ever painted – and not only during the Renaissance.

At the centre of the legend is the Emperor Constantine's dream predicting that he would defeat Maxentius if he carried the cross into battle with him. *Constantine's Dream* was the first ever night scene in painting. Piero's simplicity of structure, controlled use of perspective and the aura of serenity his work conveys are all most striking here.

Further along the Corso, past the jeweller's shops – Arezzo is the most important centre of the goldsmith trade in Italy, the 12th-century ★★ **Pieve di Santa Maria** ❷ comes into view. It is one of the most beautiful Romanesque structures in all Tuscany, with a particularly interesting facade: the central portal is flanked by five blind arcades supporting three tiers of colonnades, so that the

42

Taking in the sights

Pieve di Santa Maria

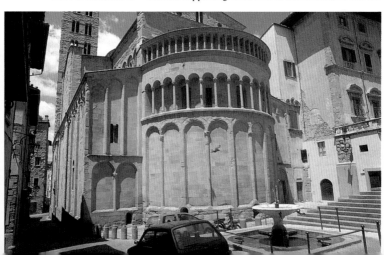

number of pillars increases towards the top, from 12 to
24 to 32. The sheer number of pillars and capitals is reminiscent of several churches in Pisa and Lucca. This is one
of the most impressive facades in Italy.

From here it's a short walk past several very medieval-
looking shops to the ★ **Piazza Grande ❸**, centre of town
life since the 13th century and scene of the *Giostra del
Saracino*, a historic jousting tournament (*see Festivals
& Folklore, page 82*). Despite the very dissimilar buildings – or perhaps because of them – the square has a special grandiose harmony of its own. Next to the
imaginatively arcaded apse of the Pieve is the 17th-cen-
tury Palazzo del Tribunale, with the little ★ **Palazzo della
Fraternità dei Laici ❹** beside it. The Gothic ground floor
(1375–77) was given an Early Renaissance first floor in
1434 by Bernardo Rossellino, and the two make a highly
attractive combination, rounded off nicely by a balcony
(1460). The tower is by Vasari, as is the grandiose
★ **Palazzo delle Logge ❺** which dates from 1573.

Piazza Grande

Back on the Corso Italia, almost at the top, is the **birthplace of Petrarch ❻**. Francesco Petrarca (1304–74) is
one of the three greatest Italian poets alongside Dante and
Boccaccio. His poems addressed to Laura, an idealised
beloved, contributed to the Renaissance flowering of lyric
poetry, and his deep interest in classical authors and the
legacy of antiquity made him Italy's first great humanist.

At the very top of the Corso there are some pleasantly
shady trees, and also a kiosk that sells cool drinks. Through
the **Municipal Park ❼** lie the remains of the **Medici
Fortress ❽** and a fantastic panoramic view, dominated
by a monumental statue of Petrarch erected during the
Fascist era.

The real highlight of Arezzo's Gothic ★ **Cathedral ❾**
are its ★ **stained-glass windows**. The work of French artist
Guillaume de Marcillat, they were created between 1518
and 1524 (de Marcillat also worked in other churches here,
notably San Francesco and SS Annunziata). The large
round window in the facade, depicting the *Miracle of Whit-
sun*, and especially the windows showing the *Raising of
Lazarus* and the *Expulsion of Moneychangers from the
Temple* are masterpieces. The cathedral also contains a
painting by Piero della Francesca: the valuable ★ **fresco
of St Mary Magdalene**, beside the door to the sacristy.
This work can usually be contemplated in comparative
peace, unlike the frescoes in San Francesco. The impressive tomb next to it was commissioned by the bishop
Guido Tarlati for himself (1328); the 16 reliefs show various glorious scenes from his life, including the capture of
several castles for the city-state of Arezzo. The 'Cappella della Madonna del Conforto' looks authentically ancient, but was in fact added at the end of the 18th century;

Arrezo's cathedral

San Domenico

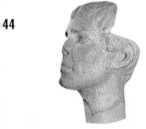
Archaeological museum exhibit

the magnificent terracotta medallions by Andrea della Robbia are genuine, however.

One of the most impressive mendicant order churches in Tuscany is the church of ★ **San Domenico** ⑩, which was begun in the Gothic style in 1275. Go through the modern portico and pretty Romanesque portal; the single-aisled interior is wonderfully bright and unpretentious. The frescoes were executed during the 14th and 15th centuries, and the ★ **crucifix** above the main altar is a fine early work by Cimabue (1272–1302).

★ **Vasari's House** ⑪ (daily 9am–7pm) is at Via XX Settembre 55. Giorgio Vasari, who was born in Arezzo in 1511 and died in Florence in 1574, was one of the most famous art historians of all time. His biographies of painters, sculptors and architects were the first scientific works of their kind. Vasari worked as a painter and architect in his home town of Arezzo, to which he remained very attached even after his move to Florence. As the chief architect and confidant of Grand Duke Cosimo I, he exerted a powerful influence on the artistic tastes of his time, and also designed several important buildings, notably the Uffizi in Florence. Vasari bought this Arezzo house in 1540 and decorated several of the rooms himself with allegorical and mythological scenes in the Mannerist style of his time.

There are two other good museums in Arezzo: the ★ **Museo Medievale e Moderno**, housed inside the 15th-century Palazzo Bruni, Via Garibaldi (daily 9am–7pm), and the **Archaeological Museum** inside the Convento di San Bernardo, Via Margaritone (Tuesday to Friday 9am–2pm, Sunday 9am–1pm).

Excursions from Arezzo

The *Casentino* is the name given to the upper part of the Arno Valley between the mountain ridges of the Pratomagno in the west and the Serra and Catenaia Alps to the east. This part of Tuscany, far from mass tourism, is covered with thick forests of chestnut trees, and the temperatures in summer are usually very pleasant. Ideally, a trip here should be combined with visits to the famous monasteries of La Verna and Camaldoli, and to attractive towns like Poppi or Stia.

Leave Arezzo on the N71 in a northerly direction, and turn off in Bibbiena. The monastery of **La Verna** lies at an altitude of 1,129m (3,704ft) above sea-level, in the middle of an ancient forest of pine and beech. It was here that St Francis of Assisi received his stigmata in the year 1224.

The small, isolated village of **Caprese**, famous as the birthplace of Michelangelo is a short drive away (34km/21 miles), and has some fine views.

The Carthusian monastery of **Camaldoli** was founded by Romuald (952–1027) – whose ascetic lifestyle impressed no less a person than the emperor Otto III – in the middle of the splendid ★ **forest of Camaldoli**. The old pharmacy contains several magnificent 16th-century cupboards and jars, and the monks' liqueur can be tasted there. Two kilometres (1 mile) further uphill is the **hermitage** *(Eremo)*, formerly inhabited by the Carthusian monks.

Excursion to Cortona

In the fertile Chiana Valley lies the pleasant little town of ★ **Cortona** (pop. 22,500), originally founded in the 7th century BC by the Etruscans. Several archaeological finds from that time are on display in the town's fascinating **Museo dell'Accademia Etrusca** (daily except Monday 10am–1pm and 4–7pm; October to March 9am–1pm and 3–5pm) in the Palazzo Pretorio, including the famous 16-armed ★ **bronze Etruscan chandelier** made in the 5th century BC, weighing almost 60 kilos, Egyptian mummies and a Lombard brooch.

Ice-cream delights

The best place to sit in the Piazza della Repubblica is on the magnificent staircase with its view of the battlemented tower of the Palazzo Comunale. From here, take a stroll across to the wonderfully peaceful Piazza della Pescaia in the picturesque upper part of the town. The romantically situated 15th-century church of San Nicolò has an elegant portico outside and a very fine coffered ceiling inside. At the very top of the hill, a steep path lined with cypresses leads up to the rather bombastic-looking church of Santa Margherita, consecrated to the town's patron saint; the panoramic ★ **view** from up here is quite unforgettable, though, and extends as far as Lake Trasimeno.

Fresco in Diocesan Museum

Cortona's most famous son is the painter Luca Signorelli, born here in 1441. His works are on display in the Diocesan Museum (daily except Monday 9.30am–1pm, 3.30–7pm, October to March 10am–1pm, 3–5pm). The **Stations of the Cross** by the Cortonese artist, Severini (1883–1966) are also worth a look.

The most attractive church in Cortona, ★ **Madonna del Calcinaio**, is actually 2km (1 mile) out of town in the direction of Camucia. This superbly elegant Renaissance building, constructed between 1485 and 1513 according to plans by Francesco di Giorgio Martini, has a beautiful light grey-and-white interior.

Madonna del Calcinaio

Those eager to stay in Tuscany at this point can take a roundabout but scenic route which connects with Route 11 (*see page 71*): travel via the Romanesque ★ **Abbey of Farneta** (near Foiano della Chiana) and then continue via the peaceful towns of Lucignano, Sinalunga and Torrita di Siena to Montepulciano (*see page 74*).

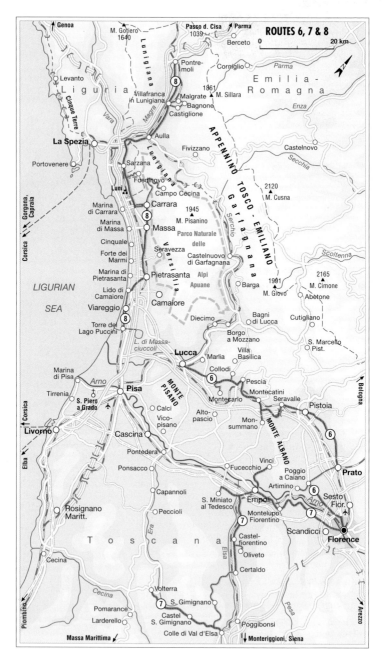

Route 6

Medici Villa in Poggio

Off the beaten Tuscan track

This route leads from Florence to Lucca via Prato and Pistoia, two towns that aren't usually included among the 'classic' destinations of any trip to Tuscany. Along the edge of the Apennines there are numerous small mountain towns and villages waiting to be discovered, such as Seravalle Pistoiese, Montecatini Alto or Buggiano Castello, along with some magnificent pulpits, elegant Medici villas and the Pinocchio Park.

Leave Florence along the N66 in the direction of Pistoia. The pleasant town of **Poggio a Caiano** (pop. 8,000) is famous for its ★ **Medici Villa** (daily 9am–3.30pm, longer in the summer, closed 2nd and 3rd Monday in the month). Lorenzo the Magnificent had this country retreat rebuilt for him from 1480. Very much in the spirit of antiquity he stressed the virtues of *otium cum dignitate* – leisure, contemplation, relaxation from the stress of everyday life in Florence, philosophical conversation and banqueting were all the major priorities. The architect, Giuliano da Sangallo, based his design on Tuscan country houses. The portico and the gable are the only ostentatious features; this was the first time since antiquity that a secular building had displayed similar architecture, and much later work was based on it. The magnificent grounds contain a delightful lemon garden *(Limonia)*. During the festival held here on the third weekend in September, the fine Monte Albano wines from Carmignano can be sampled; tasty food and also an antiques fair round off the celebrations.

Embrace the Medici philosophy

Delight in the lemon garden

La Ferndinanda

From Poggio a Caiano don't miss making a detour to **Artimino** and to ★ **La Ferdinanda**, the magnificently-situated hunting-lodge of Medici Grand Duke Ferdinand I. The landscape here is idyllic, and there is also a very good archaeological museum in the basement of the villa (weekdays except Wednesday 9am–1pm, Sunday 9am–12.30pm). *La Ferdinanda* is also known as the 'villa of a hundred chimneys', and the *paggeria* (where the pages used to live) today houses a luxury hotel with a congress centre; several houses in the village have been converted into rustic apartments as part of the hotel. Products from the *fattoria*, such as olive-oil or the superb *Carmignano* DOCG wine, can be sampled here. The restaurant, also housed in a building dating from the Medici era, serves excellent Tuscan cuisine.

Carry on across the wonderfully scenic hilly landscape around Carmignano, as far as ★ **Prato** (pop. 168,000). Though often ignored by visitors to Tuscany, Prato's ancient centre, still completely surrounded by its mighty 14th-century wall, has several unique art treasures.

The town's economy has always been linked with the textile trade, and the wool industry in particular. Cloth from Prato was in great demand right across Europe during the 13th century, and today the town is still Italy's most important textile centre. The activities of this traditional yet broad-minded town are documented in the **Museo del Tessuto** (being shifted elsewhere at present) with its valuable materials and looms and also the ★ **Museo Luigi Pecci** (daily except Tuesday 10am–7pm; note that all museums in Prato are closed on Tuesday), the largest contemporary art museum in the whole of Italy.

Prato's ★★ **cathedral**, built in 1211 in the Pisan-Lucchesan style, has an eye-catching ★ **external pulpit**, the *Pulpit of the Sacred Girdle* (1428–38 by Michelozzo). Its reliefs, with the dancing putti by Donatello, are regarded as being among the finest works of the Renaissance. Inside the cathedral is one of the most important Early Renaissance fresco cycles: the main choir chapel contains Filippo Lippi's ★ **paintings** of scenes from the lives of St John the Baptist (right) and St Stephen, one of the fathers of the church.

The ★ **Cathedral Museum** (daily except Tuesday 9.30am–12.30pm and 3–6.30pm, Sunday 9am–12.30pm) should also be visited, and not only for the original reliefs from Donatello's outdoor pulpit: the museum also provides access to the delightful 12th-century Roman-Byzantine cloister and the fascinating crypt.

Continue this tour of Prato now via the elegant Via Manzoni. The Via Accademia, which branches off it, has a very good Tuscan restaurant, 'Baghino', at No 9.

Pulpit of the Sacred Girdle

The **Piazza del Comune** contains an attractive Bacchus Fountain (1659) and also a statue of one of Prato's wealthy merchants, Francesco Datini (1330–1410), whose extensive archives, housed in Prato's **Palazzo Datini** on the Via Rinaldesca, constitute a unique record of medieval economic life. The neo-Classical facade of the **Palazzo Comunale** looks light and airy in contrast to the massive **Palazzo Pretorio** opposite.

The statue of Datini

Along the Via Cairoli stands one off Prato's finest churches, ★ **Santa Maria delle Carceri**. It was built by Giuliano da Sangallo between 1484 and 1495 on a Greek-cross ground-plan. This elegant building with its harmonious forms inside and out is considered one of the most successful examples of High Renaissance architecture. It also contains some magnificent terracotta work by Andrea della Robbia (1492).

The ★ **Castello dell'Imperatore**, built in 1248 by Frederick II, looks a bit out of place; it's actually the only Hohenstaufen castle of its kind in northern and central Italy. The church of **San Francesco** is just a few paces further on. This Gothic building was begun in 1294, and houses the tomb of the famous merchant Datini (1411) as well as an attractive 15th-century cloister and chapter house (frescoes by Niccolò Gerini).

49

There is a fascinating Fresco Museum (daily except Tuesday 9am–noon), in the pretty cloister of the church of San Domenico.

Fresco by Gerini

Souvenir hunters should note that the delightful **Fabbrica di Cantuccini**, where the famous Prato *cantuccini* are made, is very close by, at Via Ricasoli 20–22; they're traditionally sold in blue presentation boxes and bags.

The route continues now from Prato through olive groves, via Montemurlo, Montale and Santomato in the direction of Pistoia. Several establishments along this stretch of the Chianti route have signs up saying *vendita diretta*, which means wine and olive oil can be purchased direct from the producer.

Along the road from Prato

The town of ★ **Pistoia** (pop. 89,000), situated between the foothills of the Apennines and Monte Albano, is an astonishingly lively place. The people are really friendly, the shops are excellent and the sights are first-class. The local grocery stores stock all the specialities of Pistoia province: olive oil, wine, cheese and salami.

Pistoia was founded by the Romans. It prospered economically and culturally after achieving communal autonomy in 1115, and the magnificent Romanesque churches with their fine pulpits date from this period (★ **San Bartolomeo in Pantano**, ★ **Sant'Andrea** by Giovanni Pisano and ★ **San Giovanni Fuorcivitas**). However, squabbles between Guelphs and Ghibellines weakened Pistoia to

The baptistery door

The Duomo

Medallion on the
Ospedale del Ceppo

such an extent that it fell under the protection of Florence from 1324 onwards.

Anyone entering Pistoia's Cathedral Square on a Wednesday or a Saturday may miss the marvellous ★ **Baptistery** because of all the bustle of the market; this beautiful octagonal structure was built between 1338 and 1359 and based on designs by Andrea Pisano. Construction work on the ★★ **Duomo** began in Pisan Romanesque style in 1108. The porch in front of the arcaded facade was added in the 14th century. The most important work of art in the Duomo can be seen in the Chapel of St James, the famous ★ **silver altar**. This masterpiece with its 628 relief figures was created by medieval silversmiths between 1287 and 1546.

The ★ **Palazzo del Comune** is connected to the Duomo; construction work began on it in 1294. Its frescoed chambers contain the **Museo Civico** (daily except Monday 10am–7pm, Sunday and public holidays 9am–12.30pm; combined ticket for the Museo Civico, Museo Marini and Rospigliosi-Nuevo Museo Diocesano; Saturday afternoon free), which has a selection of every epoch in Pistoian art, including contemporary work. The Giovanni Michelucci Documentation Centre provides a fascinating insight into Italian 20th-century architecture. The architect Michelucci (1891–1990) was born in Pistoia, and was responsible for designing the famous church by the motorway at Campi Bisenzio.

Behind the Palazzo Comunale to the left is the ★ **Ospedale del Ceppo**. In the 16th century, the Della Robbia workshop was commissioned to do the medallions and the enamelled terracotta frieze here, which depict the seven works of mercy.

The medieval Via di Straccheria, which branches off the Via Roma, has a lot of atmosphere with its old shops. The Piazza della Sala, picturesque enough as it is, has even more character whenever the market is held here.

The richly ornamented church of ★★ **San Giovanni Fuorcivitas** is a few steps away. Work on it began as long ago as the 8th century. Its most important works of art include the ★ **stoup** by Giovanni Pisano, with the four heads of the cardinal virtues, and also the magnificent ★ **pulpit** (1270) by Fra Guglielmo da Pisa.

The rather unassuming-looking ★ **Chiesa del Tau** has a surprisingly colourful interior, entirely frescoed with scenes from the life of Sant'Antonio Abate. The former convent next to the church contains a museum devoted to the work of the sculptor Marino Marini (1901–80), who was born in Pistoia (Centro Marini: Tuesday to Saturday 9am–1pm and 3–7pm, Sunday 9am–12.30pm).

To round off this tour of Pistoia, take a look at the Palazzo Azzolini in the Via Roma (now a bank). Inside it looks just like a 15th-century palazzo but it is, in fact, a copy.

Pistoia is an ideal starting-point for hiking or mountain-biking trips into the mountains. There's also a pleasant zoo about 4km (2½ miles) out of town, the 'Città di Pistoia', Via Pieve a Celle 160 (daily 9am–sunset).

Leave Pistoia on the N435 in the direction of Lucca, and drive to **Serravalle Pistoiese** (pop. 9,000). This mini-version of San Gimignano (*see page 55*) is a magnificently-situated mountain town with an intact medieval centre and several very well-preserved *case-torri* (towers). The campanile of the 13th-century parish church of Santo Stefano was once part of the former fortifications, as was the Barbarossa Tower behind the church. The picturesque ruin of the *rocca* can be seen a short distance below the town; the hexagonal travertine tower in the olive grove looks peaceful today. The towers can also be climbed, although the panoramic view can be enjoyed just as much without the extra effort.

The next town on the route is ★ **Montecatini Terme** (pop. 20,500), one of the most prestigious spa resorts in Europe. The magnificent thermal baths here were built at the turn of the century and are still very popular. The most famous is probably Tettuccio. The upper part of the town contains a marvellous mixture of art nouveau hotels and magnificent parks and gardens.

The trip from Montecatini Terme up to **Montecatini Alto** can be made either by car or the more romantic

Montecatini Terme

52

funicular railway (April to October). Montecatini Alto is a superbly-situated walled mountain village with a magnificent view, and its main piazza is the ideal place in which to sit outside and soak in the medieval atmosphere.

The spa resort of **Monsummano Terme** (pop. 18,800), Montecatini Terme's little sister, certainly has a special flair of its own despite being rather less elegant. The grottoes here with their vapour baths are up to 300m (984ft) long, and temperatures often hover around the healthy 34°C mark (93°F). The Renaissance *loggie* on the Collegiata and the Pilgrims' Hospice are among the highlights in the town itself.

Another very fine old mountain town to visit is **Buggiano Castello**, with its fantastic view of the surrounding countryside. The central square is rather stern and forbidding, and is dominated by the austerely elegant Palazzo Pretorio.

At the centre of the Nievole Valley is the small town of **Pescia** (pop. 18,100), also known as the 'flower town of Tuscany' – there are over 1,200 flower businesses here. The *Mercato dei Fiori* (flower market) early in the morning is a real feast for the eyes. The River Nievole divides the left-hand side of the town with the cathedral square from the right-hand, secular side. The baroque cathedral and the church of **Maria Magdalena**, built in the same style, also merit a look, as does the Gothic church of **San Francesco** higher up.

The buildings making up the secular town centre are grouped around the ★ **Piazza Mazzini** on the right bank of the river; the houses and palazzi date from the 14th to 19th centuries. Highlights include the Palazzo Comunale and the pretty Renaissance church of SS Pietro e Paolo, also known as the **Madonna di Pie di Piazza**. The wooden ceiling (1605) inside showing St Peter and Paul and also the Madonna with Child is quite remarkable.

The route continues now from Pescia to **Collodi**, birthplace of Carlo Lorenzini, the author of *Pinocchio*. The nearby **Pinocchio Park** is perfect for children, and for grown-ups too because it also contains the excellent 'Osteria del Gambero Rosso'. Pinocchio's not the only attraction in Collodi: the magnificent gardens of the **Villa Garzoni**, beneath the medieval upper section of the town, are also well worth a visit.

On the way to Lucca there's a rewarding detour to the small mountain town of **Montecarlo**. It's not so much the medieval walls here but the incredibly delicious DOCG wine (red or white) that makes this place so special. At the beginning of September, there's a wine fair at which a number of gastronomic delights can also be sampled.

Route 7

Down by the river

The familiar and the not-so-familiar (*see map p46*)

This route leads from Florence to the traditional Tuscan destinations of San Gimignano and Volterra, but also includes several less well-known places like Montelupo, San Miniato, Castelfiorentino, Certaldo or Colle di Val d'Elsa. Alongside the numerous cultural sights of the medieval towns, the natural scenery on this route is often breathtaking: the famous 'classic' Tuscan landscape between San Gimignano and Volterra, and the less familiar river-valleys of the Arno and the Elsa. It's also possible to drive on from Volterra to Massa Marittima and the sea.

53

The classic Tuscan landscape

Leave Florence on the N67 and travel through the scenic landscape of the Arno Valley via Lastra a Signa to **Montelupo Fiorentino** (pop. 10,100); this town has the best ceramics museum in Tuscany (combined tickets for museums in Montelupo, Empoli and Vinci). Inside the Palazzo del Podestà is the very well laid-out ★ **Museo Archeologico e della Ceramica** (Tuesday to Sunday 9am–noon and 2.30–7pm). The ceramics museum also provides a good introduction to various glazing techniques used over the centuries. The impressive exhibits here range from antiquity to pottery created in Montelupo's successful medieval workshops, which flourished from the end of the 14th century onwards. A good time to buy pottery souvenirs here is in June, during the *Fiesta delle Ceramiche.*

Ceramics are good buys

The small but important industrial town of **Empoli** (pop. 43,500) has unfortunately paid little attention to preserving its historic buildings. The damage wrought by World War II left only three churches intact: the ★ **Collegiata Sant'Andrea** with its wonderful Romanesque facade, Santo Stefano and Santa Maria a Ripa.

The view from San Miniato

Veterans of the times

The little town of ★★ **Vinci** (pop. 13,700) isn't far away. Its most famous son, Leonardo (1452–1519), was born here illegitimately and simply tacked the name of the town on to his name: da Vinci, from Vinci.

The road leading to the medieval town centre with its olive groves and vineyards is pretty, and the centre of Vinci is still dominated by the castle of the counts of Guidi, just as it was in the 12th century. Inside the castle the authorities have set up a ★★ **Leonardo da Vinci Museum** (daily 9am–6.30pm) in honour of the great man, and the exhibits here make it clear how varied Leonardo's genius was. Around 50 scale models of his inventions have been assembled for the first time from the plans he left, including a parachute, a flying machine, flippers for swimming, diving suits, water-skis and a chain-driven bicycle. Many of these prototypes had to be 're-invented' centuries after Leonardo's death.

The tower (Tuesday to Sunday 10am–noon and 3–6pm) in **San Miniato al Tedesco** (pop. 26,000) can be seen from afar; it forms part of the *rocca* built by Frederick II, and is definitely worth climbing for the magnificent view from the top. San Miniato used to be the junction of the *Via Francigena* (the old road across the Apen-nines from Emilia into Tuscany) and the important Pisa–Florence connection. There was also a bridge over the Arno here, and the nearby hill provided a good view of what was happening down in the valley.

This strategically favourable site determined the town's fortunes historically. The Emperor Otto I made San Miniato the seat of the Imperial Vicariate in Tuscany. The castle was built by the German emperor Frederick II Hohenstaufen (hence the *al tedesco* suffix of the town's name), but little remains of it today apart from the tower, which had to be rebuilt after it was blown up by German officers during World War II.

The Prato del Duomo, a tree-lined square with a fine view, is the religious and secular centre of the town; the Romanesque facade of the Duomo stands opposite the official seat of the Inperial Vicariate, built in the 12th century. The cathedral's three-aisled interior, given a baroque face-lift during the 18th and 19th centuries, is not all that special architecturally, but the church does have one unusual feature: its elegant pulpit and several of the artistically-designed sepulchral slabs in the side-aisles were created by the modern Florentine sculptress Amalia Dupré (1845–1928).

Ceiling of the Duomo

Gourmets should take note of the fact that San Miniato al Tedesco is the 'truffle capital' of Tuscany, and a visit here in November can be an unforgettable experience (*see Festivals & Folklore, page 83*).

The tree-lined N429 leads up the Elsa Valley now to **Castelfiorentino** (pop. 17,000) which, as the name makes clear, became a Florentine castle in 1149. The main sights here are the ★ **frescoes** by Benozzo Gozzoli (1420–97) in the Biblioteca Comunale Vallesiana at Via Tilli 41 (Tuesday, Thursday and Saturday 4–7pm, Sunday 10am– noon and 4–7pm). Two magnificently restored and colourful fresco cycles have been on display in the small museum since 1986. Here the masterful work of this Florentine painter can be admired at eye-level, rather than peered at high up in a church vault.

Just beyond Castelnuovo a road branches off to the left to the ★ **Castello di Oliveto**, which today houses an *Azienda Agricola*. This marvellous fortified country house, built by a Florentine merchant in the 15th century, can simply be visited – but it's also possible to rent an apartment, taste (and buy) the wine of the house, and also eat here, if you reserve in advance (tel: 0571-64322, fax: 61508).

Certaldo (pop. 16,000) is where Giovanni Boccaccio (1313–75) died, and he may also have been born here. His *Decameron* is one of the most important works of Italian literature; its 100 stories convey a vivid and often earthy impression of Italian society in the 14th century. All the main sights of Certaldo lie on the main street in the upper, medieval part of the town: the Casa del Boccaccio, where the author spent part of his later years; the church of SS Michele e Jacopo, where he is buried; and the attractive Palazzo Pretorio. It is worth walking to the very top – to the 'Osteria del Vicario', housed inside an 11th-century canonry at Via Rivellino 3, with its excellent Tuscan cuisine, superb view and Romanesque cloister.

A delightful stretch of road full of bends leads to the most important town in the Elsa Valley, ★★ **San Gimignano** (pop. 7,000). It once had 72 medieval *case-*

55

Tuscany in bloom

torri (towers), and the 13 that still remain, when observed from a distance, are reminiscent of the Manhattan skyline. These towers often resembled small fortresses in their own right, and were very necessary whenever rival families fought one another.

San Gimignano town once lay on the *Via Francigena* (the old road across the Apennines from Emilia into Tuscany); the Via San Matteo and Via San Giovanni follow the old route. Pilgrims and merchants visiting the town from foreign lands paid for accommodation and souvenirs, and in this way San Gimignano gradually grew rich and prosperous. However, the loss of the trade route in the 14th century led to an economic and political crisis. San Gimignano grew impoverished, the money for its ambitious building projects was suddenly no longer available, and the structures dating from the 11th and 12th centuries have hardly been altered at all since they were built.

These days, winter is the only time that visitors here can still sense something of the contemplative atmosphere of past centuries. Since it received UNESCO funds for restoration of its buildings, San Gimignano has been experiencing something of a miniature economic boom; it has now developed into a leading tourist attraction, and is usually overfull, especially during the summer. There are special combination discount admission tickets available for all the municipal museums (April to September Tuesday to Sunday 9.30am–12.30pm and 3–6pm, October to March 9.30am–12.30pm and 2.30–5.30pm).

Piazza della Cisterna

The ★ **Piazza della Cisterna** is the real heart of the town. The square was named after the well that was built here in 1273, and is at its most atmospheric early in the morning or late in the evening when the tourists are absent. Just beyond the piazza is the cathedral square, another splendid sight. The loggia on the facade of the ★ **Palazzo del Popolo** (completed 1288) is one of the oldest in Tuscany; at 54m (177ft) the tower is the highest in the town.

Fresco in the Collegiata

The ★ **Collegiata Santa Maria Assunta** was begun in the Romanesque style, and contains some marvellous medieval fresco cycles; inside, there are themes from the New Testament on the right-hand wall, and from the Old Testament on the left, painted by Sienese artists during the 14th century.

The Via San Matteo leads from the cathedral square, past distinctive-looking houses and towers, to the Gothic church of ★ **Sant'Agostino**. The main choir chapel holds a surprise in store: 17 fine frescoes by Benozzo Gozzoli, depicting scenes from the life of St Augustine.

Leave San Gimignano now and drive towards Colle di Val d'Elsa. The landscape along this rather sinuous route is attractive at any season: it's a brilliant green in the spring, full of golden-yellow fields of corn in the summer, or dark clods of earth in the autumn.

★ **Colle di Val d'Elsa** (pop. 17,500) is probably the most pleasant of Tuscany's many small medieval mountain towns. The townspeople grew wealthy and built several palazzi. Minerals were mined in this area as long ago as Etruscan times, and during the Middle Ages the town also grew rich from wool, silk and paper manufacture. The River Elsa provided the necessary water for the paper industry, and the quality of the paper was so good that one of the first ever printing centre in Italy was set up in Colle di Val d'Elsa in 1478. Glass is also an important industry here (a good place for glassware souvenirs in Colle is the shop at Via del Castello 5).

Floral hues

Today, industry in Colle is located in the lower part of town; the ★ **upper town** has thus managed to retain its intact medieval character. The impressive 16th-century fortification walls at the ★ **Porta Nuova** controlled access to the Borgo. Access to the fortress itself is via the ★ **Palazzo Campana**; its richly-ornamented facade is typical of the architectural style of the 16th century. A highlight among the medieval streets is the Via delle Volte, which is completely roofed over.

57

By way of contrast there's a striking building in the lower part of town that may not be to everyone's taste: the adventurous modern structure, noticeably red-coloured among the old wool and paper factories, houses the local branch of the Monte dei Paschi bank, and was built by the Pistoian architect Michelucci.

The yellow-and-grey landscape and clay hills along the road to ★★ **Volterra** (pop. 12,000) have a special austere beauty of their own, as does the town itself. Volterra's strategically favourable location on a hilltop above the confluence of the Cecina and the Era persuaded the Etruscans to build their city of *Velethri* on the site, and it grew to become one of the most powerful cities in the Etruscan Confederation. During the Middle Ages the city became a free commune (12th century). In 1361 it was placed under Florentine rule, which it never managed to shake off completely, despite several uprisings. Volterra merits a visit, not only for its historic medieval buildings but also for its craft workshops, where the antique art of working alabaster has been practised since the 18th century.

Craftsman at work
Medallions on the Palazzo dei Priori

The ★ **Piazza dei Priori** is marvellously austere, much like many other parts of Volterra; the Palazzo dei Priori on the square, built between 1208 and 1254, is the oldest-preserved communal palace in Tuscany, and served as model for the Palazzo Vecchio in Florence. The vestibule with the coat-of-arms of the *podestà* is definitely worth seeing, as are the state rooms on the first floor.

A few steps away is Volterra's ★★ **Cathedral**. Its three-aisled interior lost its Romanesque character during the 16th century when the magnificent coffered ceiling was added. There's a real masterpiece of Romanesque wood-carving here: the 13th-century ★ *Deposition* in the right transept, with life-sized figures in polychrome wood. The delightful reliefs on the pulpit and also the two charming terracotta groups in the 'Cappella dell'Addolorata' warrant closer inspection, as does the marvellous *Adoration of the Magi* fresco in the same chapel painted by Benozzo Gozzoli.

The Deposition

An important collection of over 600 Etruscan cinerary urns can be admired at the ★★ **Museo Etrusco Guarnacci** (winter 9am–2pm, 16 March to 1 November 9am–7pm). They provide a unique insight into Etruscan art. The famous *urna degli sposi* (urn of the married couple) shows how realistic Late Etruscan art became; the bronze votive figure known as the *shadow of the evening* is no less famous, and dates from the 3rd century BC. Special combination discount admission tickets are available for the Museo Etrusco and the art gallery in the Palazzo Minucci Solaini (March to October 9.30am–1pm and 3–6.30pm, otherwise morning only).

Etruscan sculpture

Volterra is dominated at its highest point by the **Fortezza**, a magnificent example of Renaissance military architecture. Today it serves as a prison. High on the hilltop, on the site of the former Etruscan acropolis, is the Archeological Park, an ideal place for a picnic.

The upper section of the imposing Etruscan town gate known as the ★ **Porta all'Arco** is actually Roman, but the massive pieces of square-cut masonry at the base of the structure are relics from the original Etruscan gate, built in the 4th century BC. There are several alabaster workshops in the street leading up to the gate. Exhibitions of local alabaster products can be visited in the Via Turazza and also on the Piazza dei Priori. The Porta Fiorentina leads to the excavated **Roman Theatre**, built during the reign of Augustus, and also the 3rd-century Roman Baths.

The Roman Theatre

The very steep precipice known as *Le Balze* (outside the Porta San Francesco) was formed by natural erosion; San Giusto was swallowed up in 1895, and the ravine continues to threaten the houses near its edge.

From Volterra it's possible either to take the N68 along the Cecina Valley and on to the sea, or opt for the scenically stunning but rather curvaceous N439 via Pomarance and **Larderello** to Massa Marittima *(see page 65)*. A sudden odour of bad eggs indicates that Larderello's sulphur springs aren't far away.

For those interested, Larderello also has a museum documenting the use of geothermic energy (daily on request 8am–5pm).

Route 8

Mountain Peaks and Sandy Beaches (*see map p46*)

This route leads through the Lunigiana, a region completely untouched by tourism, from Pontremoli to Pietrasanta via Carrara and Massa. Another option would be to take the coast road beyond Aulla and travel from Marina di Carrara to Torre del Lago Puccini via Viareggio.

The Lunigiana comprises the valley of the River Magra and its tributaries, and got its name from the Roman colony of Luni in Liguria; its Roman amphitheatre still exists and can be seen at the Luni Archaeological Site. This border region between Emilia-Romagna, Liguria and Tuscany was ruled by several small families from the nobility. They supervised travellers and goods passing along the *Via Francigena*, the old road across the Apennines from Emilia into Tuscany which crossed their territory. There are more castles in the region of Lunigiana than anywhere else in Tuscany.

Thanks to its strategically favourable situation on the Via Francigena during medieval times, **Pontremoli** (pop. 8,700), south of the Cisa Pass, is still the gateway to Tuscany today. Its old town is picturesquely situated on a spit of land at the confluence of the Magra and Verde rivers. The state of the two towers in the town centre (one of which is the campanile of the cathedral) illustrates the ferocity of the various inter-party battles fought during the Middle Ages. The towers originally formed part of a wall erected by Castruccio Castracani in 1322 to separate the Guelfs in the upper part of the town from the Ghibellines in the lower part.

59

Bathing near Pontremoli

The main square in Pontremoli

It's worth climbing up to the *castello*, because it houses the fascinating ★ **Museo delle Statue-Stele** (June to September Tuesday to Sunday 9am–noon and 4–7pm, October to May 9am–noon and 2–5pm); the statues here date back to around 2000BC and are otherwise only found in the Alpine valleys to the north. This archaic cult seems to have lasted a very long time in the Lunigiana: an inscription dating from AD752 mentions the destruction of idols and conversion of the heathens.

Old town embellishment

Pontremoli is a good starting-point for hiking trips to the various mountain peaks of the area, eg the **Foce dei tre confini**, the point 1,408m (4,619ft) above sea-level where the borders of Emilia-Romagna, Liguria and Tuscany all meet up.

There's a wonderful view of the 1,800-m (5,900-ft) high mountain peaks from the N62, which travels via Pieve de Sorano to **Villafranca in Lunigiana** (pop. 4,800). Today the *castello* of the Malespina, formerly the most powerful family in this region, is nothing more than a picturesque ruin. The Museo Etnografico della Lunigiana (Tuesday to Sunday 9am–noon and 3–6pm, summer 9am–noon, 4–7pm), situated on the edge of the old town (much of which was destroyed during the war), provides a good impression of what everyday life must have been like for the people who lived here centuries ago.

The Lunigiana region of Tuscany has a vast choice of small towns practically untouched by tourism. Particularly impressive places include Malgrate, Bagnone and Castiglione, all of which look almost like fairy-tale towns from a distance.

Travel via **Aulla**, the largest town in the Lunigiana which suffered particularly heavy damage during the war. Then take a short but worthwhile detour to the sea and ★ **Fosdinovo** (daily except Tuesday, guided tours at 10am, 11am, 4pm, 5pm and 6pm, tel: 0187-68891), one of the finest Malaspina fortresses in the area with a magnificent view that extends as far as the Gulf of La Spezia.

The coastal region known as the *Versilia*, which stretches from Cinquale to the Lago di Massaciuccoli, has broad sandy beaches, clean water, refreshing pine forests and the Apuan Alps in the background, and is one of the most popular bathing resort areas on the Tyrrhenian Sea.

All the towns along the coast here – Marina da Carrara, Marina di Massa, Cinquale, Forte dei Marmi, Marina di Pietrasanta, Lido di Camaiore and Viareggio – have excellent tourist infrastructures, water sports facilities, nightclubs, discos, restaurants, hotels of every category and also several campsites. Viareggio, also a popular holiday destination in winter because of its famous carnival, and Forte dei Marmi are two of the more cosmopolitan resorts which have been well-known since the beginning of the century. The poet Shelley was drowned in a boating accident off Viareggio on 8 July 1822, while sailing from Livorno to La Spezia. His ashes lie in the Protestant Cemetery in Rome.

Right at the foot of the snow-peaked Apuan Alps are the spa resorts of Carrara, Massa, Pietrasanta and Camaiore. The extensive amount of high-quality marble in the Apuan Alps just here has made **Carrara** (pop. 67,000) well-known throughout history. The quarries here provided marble for the temples and statues of Ancient Rome; the Italians decorated their medieval churches with marble from Carrara; and Michelangelo came here personally – as did Henry Moore – to select sculpture blocks. Today Carrara is one of the leading exporters of marble in the world (over 800,000 tons annually). A trip to the marble quarries is an impressive experience and should be com-

Fortress at Fosdinovo

Continuing the trade of centuries

plemented by a visit to the Museo Civico del Marmo di
Carrara in the Viale XX Settembre (daily except Sunday
10am–5pm, longer in summer).

Cemetery in Carrara

Take home a piece of marble

Carrara is an ideal starting-point for several superb trips
into the Apuan Alps, since 1985 a nature conservation area.
A trip along the N446d up to Campo Cecina (1,320m/
4,330ft above sea-level) will be rewarded by a breathtaking
panoramic ★ **view** from the Gulf of La Spezia as far as
Livorno. On a clear day it is possible to see Corsica.

Like Carrara, the capital of the province, **Massa** (pop.
67,000), has only a small medieval section, with most of
the older buildings grouped around the central Piazza degli
Aranci. The imposing Renaissance castle of the Malaspina
family dominates the town. It is generally only open to
visitors during festivals.

Beyond Massa, in Seravezza, is the visitor centre for
the Apuan Alps Natural Park, which organises tours into
the mountains for hikers and riders (for more information contact Pro Loco, Via C del Greco 11, 55047 Seravezza, tel: 0584-75 72 25, fax: 75 61 44).

The central Piazza del Duomo in the old section of
Pietrasanta (pop. 25,000) is surprisingly large, and most
of the town's sights are located here. The eye-catching red
campanile stands next to the 13th-century marble Duomo.
Marble has always played a special role here: the interior of the cathedral contains several works by the sculptor Stagio Stagi (1496–1563), who was born in Pietrasanta.
One of the most interesting museums in the town also takes
marble as its theme: the Museo dei Bozzetti (October to
May, Tuesday to Thursday, Saturday 9am–noon, 2.30–
7pm, Friday 2.30–7pm, 9–11.30pm; June and September,
Tuesday to Saturday 4–7pm; July and August, Tuesday to

Botero's 'Hell'

Saturday 6–8pm, 9pm–midnight) in the harmonious cloister of the monastery of Sant'Agostino. The museum contains around 200 models and studies by many different sculptors who come here from all over the world. The church of San Martino in the Via Mazzini contains an interesting work by the 20th-century Colombian sculptor Botero: two frescoes on the theme of *Heaven and Hell*.

Drive from **Viareggio** on the coast to **Torre del Lago Puccini** (7km/4¼ miles away) on the Lago di Massaciuccoli. The villa of the composer **Giacomo Puccini**, where he wrote all his operas except for *Turandot* and also hunted, is directly next to the lake (in summer Tuesday to Sunday 10am–noon and 3.30–6pm, shorter in winter). 'Second only to the piano my favourite instrument is the rifle,' Puccini used to say fondly. He and his wife and son are buried in the chapel near the villa.

One can go back into the mountains at this point and travel into the Garfagnana region, which like the Lunigiana is relatively free of tourists. Follow the course of the River Serchio to the prettiest town in this area, **Barga** (pop. 10,200), an old medieval town perched picturesquely on top of the hill, and dominated by its Romanesque ★**Duomo**.

Barga's hilltop location
Cathedral portal

The Duomo contains a 12th-century marble pulpit carved by the sculptor, Guido Bogorelli from Como. The pillars supporting the pulpit rest on the backs of lions while the inlaid decoration and panels of the pulpit itself, on which there are scenes from the scriptures, ensures that this work takes its place among Tuscany's finest early Renaissance altars.

Route 9

Sightseeing and swimming

The bathing resorts south of Livorno – the starting-point for this route – are known collectively as the 'Etruscan Riviera'. In high summer it's less crowded than in the Versilia. The coast here is a mixture of pleasant bays and rocks overgrown with *macchia*. The route goes via Rosignano Marittimo, Massa Marittima and Grosseto to Ansedonia in the part of Tuscany known as the Maremma, with its miles-long sandy beaches and extensive pine groves.

Livorno (formerly known to the English as *Leghorn*, pop. 166,000), Tuscany's gateway to the sea, and native city of the composer Mascagni (1863–1945) and the artist Modigliani (1884–1920), was originally founded as a harbour town by Pisa. Its rapid rise to prominence as one of the most important harbours in the Mediterranean only began under Medici rule, however; it was they who built the city's fortresses, squares and canals.

Livorno was designed almost from scratch in 1575 by Buontalenti as an ideal Renaissance city, and the architect's ideas can still be made out on closer scutiny of any city map, despite the serious damage inflicted during World War II.

Today this important industrial city is characterised by its broad squares, such as the Piazza della Repubblica. Walk from here across the Via Grande, with its elegant arcaded passageways, then across the Piazza Grande with the Duomo, and over to the Piazza Micheli next to the old harbour basin. The most famous monument in Livorno can be seen here: the **Monumento dei Quattro Mori**, showing Grand Duke Ferdinand I with four Moorish slaves. The picturesque ★ **Quartiere Veneziano**, situated between Fortezza Vecchia and Fortezza Nuova, is a very good part of the city to go shopping or simply stroll about.

Those with time on their hands should use the scenic Roman road *Via Aurelia*, now better known as the N1. For those in a hurry, the motorway runs almost parallel.

ROUTE 9

Castiglioncello harbour

Florence

The small bathing resort of Quercianella is followed by the pleasantly-situated town of Castiglioncello. From Rosignano Solvay, with its almost surreal-looking industrial complex, it's worth taking a detour to **Rosignano Marittimo** (pop. 30,000). This town provides a magnificent panoramic view, and it also has a 13th-century *castello* housing an archaeological museum, which documents several of the finds made in the region.

Further south along the coast, the towns of Vada, Marina di Cecina and Forte di Bibbona all have remains of Medici fortresses.

Beyond Forte di Bibbona, the longest avenue of cypresses in Italy (4.8km/3 miles) leads to the very medieval town of **Bolgheri**, where the Italian poet and Nobel Prize-winner Giosuè Carducci (1835–1907) spent his youth from 1838 onwards. He immortalised the cypresses and the atmosphere of the place in his numerous poems.

Tuscany's symbol, the cypress tree, is suffering increasingly from a strange disease which has probably been caused by air pollution, and is characterised by thin branches, a brownish colour and a thinning-out of the foliage at the top. Many avenues leading to magnificent villas are starting to look rather forlorn, and even the famous cypresses of Bolgheri have now been replaced by a new and more sturdy variety.

Ideal for families

Follow the Via Aurelia

The nearby resort of **Marina di Castagneto-Donoratico**, with its gently-sloping beach, is ideal for family holidays. A particularly delightful stretch of road leads inland from the sea at this point. Among the hills covered with forest – nice and cool during the heat of the summer – there are several very medieval towns. The first one to appear is Castagneto Carducci (the poet Carducci lived here too, *see above*) with its castle and magnificent view across the plain sloping down towards the sea.

A well-surfaced stretch of road with several bends now leads past a series of superb views and through chestnut forests to the mountain village of Sassetta, and then on to ★ **Suvereto**. The intact medieval core of this village is just as pleasantly surprising and interesting as its Romanesque church of San Giusto, which contains some rare alabaster windows.

Coat-of-arms in Campiglia

Follow the River Cornia as far as **Campiglia Marittima** (pop. 12,600) with its 12th-century Pisan fortress, its Palazzo Pretorio (decorated with many coats-of-arms) and the Romanesque Pieve San Giovanni (outside the town on a hill next to the cemetery). The resort of **San Lorenzo** is one of the most popular on the Etruscan Riviera. Alongside the usual tourist infrastructure, it also caters for nightowls.

There's a good detour from San Lorenzo, leading through forests of oak and pine to the magnificent Gulf of Baratti. The ★ **Etruscan tumulus tombs** here can actually be entered. There's a superb view out to sea from the tiny castellated village of **Populonia**, which also has a small archaeological museum. The finds here were buried under enormous Etruscan slag heaps and are thus in very good condition. The iron industry is still important in this region today; Piombino, the centre of Tuscan heavy industry, is not far away. The town is also the port for the nearby holiday island of Elba.

In the shade at Populonia beach

Drive via Torre Mozza now to Follonica, a modern bathing resort situated at the centre of a beautiful pine grove in the Maremma. From Follonica it is a short excursion to ★ **Massa Marittima** (pop. 9,300). Massa Marittima owed its rise to prominence to two main factors: the decision to transfer the episcopal see to Massa from Populonia, and the extensive mineral deposits in the nearby *Colline Metallifere*. A period of decline set in during the 16th century after a malaria outbreak, and the mines were only reopened in the 19th century after the swamps had been successfully drained. This long phase of decline had one advantage, however: today the town still looks very much as it did back then. The *Città Vecchia* dates from the 11th to 13th centuries, and the upper, 'new' section from the 13th and 14th centuries. After that time there was no money left for any further alteration.

Massa Marittima's ★ **Piazza Garibaldi** is one of the most spectacular squares in Tuscany. It is surrounded by several magnificent buildings: the Palazzo Comunale, the Logge del Comune opposite it, the **Palazzo Pretorio** and the ★ **Duomo** all form a perfect ensemble. The cathedral was begun in the Pisan style in 1228, and completed in the Gothic style in the 14th century. The inside and the outside both merit a close look, and particularly the ★ **font** by Giroldo da Como, hewn from a single travertine block

Duomo, Massa Marittima

(1267). The Palazzo Pretorio houses an archaeological museum which exhibits finds from the surrounding area, and also an art gallery (daily except Monday 1 April to 30 September 10am–12.30pm and 3.30–7pm, 1 October to 31 March 10am–12.30pm and 3–5pm) with a very fine *Madonna* by Ambrogio Lorenzetti on display.

Symbol of the new town

The 'new town' contains the impressive remains of a Sienese fortress. There is also an interesting old oil-mill (*Antico Frantoio*). Finally, the Museo Miniera (mining museum) here and the 700-m (2,300-ft) long mining tunnel provide an insight into the methods of ore mining.

Drive along the magnificent 10-km (6-mile) long stretch of pine forest along the coast known as the 'Pineto del Tombolo', and then past Marina di Grosseto with its sandy beaches to reach **Grosseto** (pop. 71,000). This town is the largest in the Maremma, and many of its buildings are modern because of the devastation wrought here during World War II. The only structure left standing was the town's mighty wall, built during the 16th century. There's a very good museum here, the Museo Archeologico e d'arte della Maremma (Piazza Baccarini), but unfortunately it is closed for an indefinite period.

The excavations at ★ **Roselle**, one of the most important Etruscan cities in northern Etruria, are so idyllically situated in an olive grove that it's almost like being in Crete. The paved streets, the ruins of Etruscan taverns and workshops and the 3km (1.8 mile) long cyclopean wall are all very atmospheric, as are the Roman amphitheatre and the old forum.

The tumulus graves at Roselle

The nearby hilltop village of Vetulonia lies above the ancient Etruscan city of *Vetluna*, a former member of the Dodecapolis confederation. The small area that has been excavated (*Scavi Città*) is fascinating, as are the magnificent ★ **tumulus graves**.

From Grosseto, the N1 leads past the magnificent ★ **Parco Naturale dell'Uccellina**. Out of season, the unspoilt sandy beach is pleasant for swimming; in high summer things get quite crowded, the street is closed to traffic and a bus service takes bathers to the sea and back.

In Albinia it's possible to connect with Route 11 (*see page 71*) by following the extremely scenic N74, which travels via Manciano. Turn-off to the 'Terme di Saturnia' sulphur springs, which are open to the public and then on to Pitigliano (*see page 77*).

Now there's yet more fantastic landscape: a trip around the almost circular peninsula of **Monte Argentario** also provides several beautiful views out across the sea. Today this former island (highest elevation 635m/2,083ft, 12km/7

miles out to sea) is connected to the mainland by three sandy promontories. The attractive towns of Orbetello, Porto Ercole and **Porto San Stefano** (ferry connection to Giglio Island) all have ruined Spanish fortresses, because Monte Argentario was part of the Spanish-controlled Stato dei Presidi from 1555 until 1808.

The last coastal resort in Tuscany, **Ansedonia**, is also a cultural highlight: it is the site of the ancient Etruscan and Roman port of *Cosa*. The Etruscan canal that was cut through the rock here is still very impressive today, and may whet the appetite for a visit to the flat-topped hill containing the remains of the city of Cosa, or to the archaeological museum.

Maremma – derived from *Marittima* – is the name given to the hilly and swampy region which was infested by malaria after the Etruscan drainage installations decayed, and remained very unhealthy until it was finally reclaimed in the 19th century. Until 1840 the average life expectancy of the population was under 20 years. It was only when the swamps were drained in the 19th century that Tuscany's *butteri* (the local word for 'cowboys') were able to return with their herds of cattle.

The real attraction of this landscape is the combination of broad plains and hilly hinterland. There are fine views out across the sea from the various old mountain towns and villages (eg Montepescali, Magliano in Toscana or Capalbio).

The unique flora and fauna of the Maremma can best be appreciated in one of its three natural parks: the Parco Naturale dell'Uccellina, the Rifugio Faunistico Lago di Burano and the Rifugio Faunistico Laguna di Orbetello. Further information can be obtained from the visitor centre in Alberese, tel: 0564-40 70 98, or the headquarters of the WWF in Tuscany (Via Sant'Anna 3, Florence, tel/fax: 055-47 78 76).

Porto San Stefano

Enjoy the views and the flora

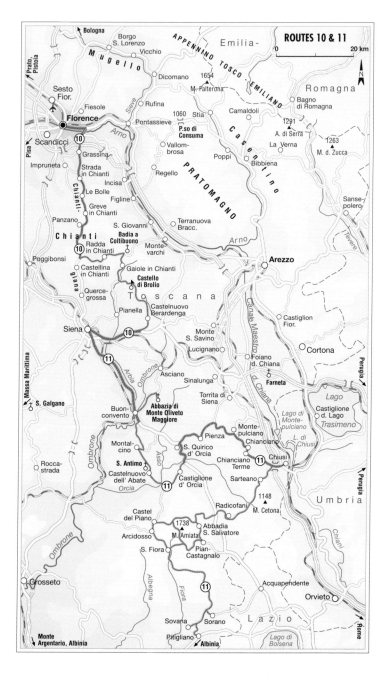

Route 10

Chianti country

The *Chiantigiana*, or N222, which connects Florence with Siena via Strada, Greve, Radda and Castellina, passes through some of the most scenic landscape in Tuscany. Isolated farmhouses, rows of cypresses along the gentle skyline, vast panoramic views, vineyards and groves of (newly-planted) olive trees – this route has all the magical Tuscan ingredients.

Chianti is probably the most famous Italian red wine; in 1984 it was given the highest distinction in Italy, DOCG (*denominazione di origine controllata e garantita*). The growers' association chose the black cockerel (*gallo nero*) as its symbol. For many years Chianti was sold in large straw bottles and had rather a cheap image; several vintners have recently been selling it as *Vino da Tavola*, and the wine has been winning new respect.

Chianti News (available at all hotels, restaurants and travel agencies) lists information about restaurants, festivals, accommodation, wine-tasting establishments and good places to shop.

Grapes of repute

Leave Florence on the N222 and travel south as far as Grassina. Beyond the town, the road begins to wind its way down to the elegant Villa Ogolino, where there is an 18-hole golf course.

On the right, just beyond Strada in Chianti, the massive tower of the Castello di Vicchomaggio comes into view. The villa itself is surrounded by cypresses and a magnificent Italian garden. The large Renaissance cellar here contains traditional Chianti but also Chardonnay and Cabernet Sauvignon (overnight accommodation also possible).

Greve in Chianti (pop. 12,000) has just one magnificent asymmetrical ★ **piazza** surrounded by arcades. There are a large number of small shops, nearly all of which sell wines, including those from the *fattoria* in the nearby *castello* in Uzzano (to get there, turn off just before Greve), and the *Mona Lisa* wines. The beautiful woman immortalised by Leonardo da Vinci was born in the Villa di Vignamaggio (in the direction of Lámole). Today the villa is a fine Renaissance structure surrounded by cypresses and statues in a festive Italian ★ **garden**. The *Riserva* wine from the *fattoria* naturally bears the name *Mona Lisa*. It's also possible to stay here overnight.

Vine culture

The town of **Panzano** lies almost on the *Chiantigiana*. Prince Alceo di Napoli Rampolla uses the Cabernet grape – unusual for Tuscany – at his Castello dei Rampolla near Santa Lucia in Faulle. The velvety red *Sammarco* is three-quarters Cabernet and one quarter Sangiovese.

Harvest time

En route to Badia

Close to the small town of Panzano is the Romanesque ★ **Pieve San Leolino**. Its elegant portico is delightful, especially at sunset.

The pretty little town of **Castellina in Chianti** lies right in the heart of the region. Besides street cafés, such as 'Il Cantuccio', there is the 'Antica Trattoria la Torre', just outside the *rocca*, which serves typical Chianti cooking and also several historic dishes.

Carry on along the *Chiantigiana* and you'll reach Siena (*see page 32*). Next on the route is a little village of captivating charm, **Radda in Chianti** (pop. 1,650). The vintners' association known as the 'Consorzio dello Gallo Nero' was founded in the Fattoria Vignale just outside the village in 1924, and since that time the black cockerel has been the symbol of the Chianti League, which has had its headquarters in Radda since 1415.

About 3km (1¾ miles) outside Radda a road leads up to **Castello di Volpaia**, a medieval village delightfully situated 600m (2,000ft) up on the wooded slopes of the Chianti Hills. The wine here is excellent, especially the *Bianco Val d'Arbia*, a fruity white.

Continue now through a wooded region to **Badia a Coltibuono**. The Romanesque abbey church with its mighty campanile was founded by monks in the 11th century; the *fattoria* produces some fine wines with a subtle aftertaste often reminiscent of strawberries or cherries.

At **Gaiole in Chianti** the landscape is stunning. The former convent of Castello di Spaltenna today houses a hotel-restaurant and wine business.

A little further south is the mighty **Castello di Brolio** (daily 9am–noon and 3–6pm, tel: 0577-74 71 04), seat of the Ricasoli family. The view from the battlements in clear weather extends as far as Monte Amiata and Siena. The 'father of modern Chianti' reigned here in the truest sense of the word: Bettino Ricasoli (1809–90) was the first prime minister of a united Italy, and his mixture of red and white grape varieties became a classic Chianti. The *Riserva del Barone*, a noble red which needs at least five years to mature, or the *Galestro* white wine are two very good Ricasoli products.

Castelnuovo Berardenga marks the end of Chianti Classico territory. The landscape alters, too: the green, forest-covered hills start to be replaced by golden yellows and greyish browns. *Crete* is the term applied to the clay ravines formed by erosion which are such a typical feature of this region south of Siena. During particularly arid summers the interlocking pale clay hummocks and treeless gullies are often reminiscent of a desert.

The town of Siena (*see page 32*) can be reached from here along the N73.

Sunflower season

Route 11

Monte Oliveto Maggiore Abbey

Plains and forests (*see map p68*)

This route follows the old *Via Cassia* from Siena, makes a detour into the hills to the monasteries of Monte Oliveto Maggiore or Sant'Antimo, the wine towns of Montalcino or Montepulciano, the Renaissance jewel of Pienza, Monte Amiata or the ancient Etruscan region around Pitigliano. The backbone of this tour, however, is the N2, which crosses one of the most scenic regions of Tuscany. In August, when the large bales of straw are drying in the freshly-harvested fields and the hot air shimmers above the hilltops, this trip can be unforgettable.

Leave Siena (*see page 32*) on the N2. The town of **Buonconvento** lies at the confluence of the Arbia and Ombrone rivers; completely enclosed by walls, it has successfully retained its medieval character.

From here drive on to the abbey of ★ **Monte Oliveto Maggiore**. Members of the Sienese nobility retired to this isolated region and founded this Benedictine abbey among the wooded hills. It has one of the finest cloisters in Tuscany; the ★ **frescoes** here are colourful, true to life and also feature some fine background landscapes. Scenes 1–20, depicting the life of St Benedict, were painted by Sodoma, and the rest of the frescoes are by Luca Signorelli. Small bottles of the excellent monastery liqueur can be purchased at the old pharmacy.

The staircase in the abbey

The town of **Montalcino** (pop. 7,000) is very picturesquely situated on a hilltop above the valleys of the Ombrone and the Asso rivers. The view from the battlements of the Sienese fortress (winter 9am–1pm, 2–6pm, summer 9am–1pm, 2.30–8pm) can be very atmospheric when the valley down below fills with fog and only a

Montalcino's Sienese fortress

Some of the best red wines

Sant'Antimo

few hilltops can be seen in the far distance. *Brunello di Montalcino* is one of the very best reds Italy has to offer. This full-bodied, aromatic, rather smoky-tasting wine is named after the dark *(bruno)* colour of the Sangiovese grape. *Brunello* has to mature for at least three years in oak vats to qualify for the DOCG label. The *Rosso di Montalcino* is also an excellent red, even though it only takes one year to mature.

The headquarters of the Montalcino vintners' association, which provides information on local *fattorie* and their wines, is in the 14th-century Palazzo Comunale (in winter 9am–1pm and 2–6pm, closed Monday; in summer 9am–1pm and 2.30–8pm) in the Piazza del Popolo. The nearby 'Caffè Fischetteria', with its turn-of-the-century atmosphere, is a good place to stop off for a quick cappuccino.

A good souvenir of Montalcino – apart from a bottle of *Brunello* – are the local green-and-white ceramic products, which can also be bought up at the fortress.

Carry on in the direction of Castelnuovo dell'Abate, to visit the unique monastery of Sant'Antimo there, and also the odd wine-cellar. Just beyond Montalcino is the Villa Greppo, the oldest vineyard in this region. A little further on there's a left-turn to the Fattoria Barbi, another traditional *Brunello* producer. The wines and products of the *fattoria* can be enjoyed in the excellent restaurant here.

★ **Sant'Antimo** is one of the most important 13th-century abbeys in Italy. According to legend the original Cistercian abbey was founded by Charlemagne, and its 12th-century Romanesque church is certainly one of the finest in Tuscany. The rich sculpture around the portal and the apses is particularly impressive, and the pillars inside have several magnificent capitals which should be examined individually. One real masterpiece is *Daniel in the Lions' Den* (second pillar on the right in the nave). Onyx or alabaster was used for some of the columns, especially in the ambulatory, and they take on an almost translucent glow when the sunlight falls on them.

The next small town on this route lies directly on the Via Cassia: **San Quirico d'Orcia** (pop. 2,400). The highlight here is the 12th-century Romanesque *Collegiata*. Notable features outside are the marvellous sculpture decoration on the portals and windows, while the interior contains an incomparable masterpiece: the ★ **choir stalls**, originally destined for Siena cathedral, with their magnificent inlay work (c 1500). The Italian Renaissance gardens known as the **Horti Leonini** are also worth seeing.

Carry on northwards along the N146, following signs to Pienza. The green fields here are particularly beautiful in the springtime, and provide good grazing for the local sheep: this region produces the famous Tuscan ewe's cheese known as *pecorino*, the speciality of ★★ **Pienza** (pop. 2,300). This town is a Renaissance jewel, situated picturesquely on a hilltop affording breathtaking, panoramic views of the surrounding countryside. The superb buildings in the centre were commissioned from the architect Bernardo Rossellino by Pius II, the Piccolomini pope, who was born here in 1405. At that time the town was still known as Corsignano; Pius II changed its name by papal bull to Pienza in 1462. The ★★ **Piazza Pio II** documents the magnificence of the project that could not be applied as planned to the entire town after the deaths of both pope and architect in 1464. The facades of the Palazzo Piccolomini, the Duomo, the canonry and the bishop's palace together form what is perhaps the most harmonious Renaissance ensemble anywhere in Italy.

Piazza Pio II in Pienza

The ★ **Duomo** looks like an antique temple from the outside (note the coat-of-arms of Pius II above), but the interior with its elegant architecture was clearly influenced by Northern European models. The whole church has had to be shored up at the east end, and is in unstable condition – note the cracks in the wall.

Vaulting in the Duomo

73

Rossellino based his design of the ★ **Palazzo Piccolomini** on Leon Battista Alberti's three-storeyed Palazzo Rucellai in Florence, and this building is considered his masterpiece. There is a magnificent view of the Orcia Valley from the Renaissance ★ **loggia**.

Nearby is a very ancient church, the ★ **Pieve di Corsignano**, probably built during the 10th century. It has some unusual carvings (including a strange double-tailed siren above the door), and the setting above the valley is idyllic.

Palazzo Piccolomini courtyard

Palazzi in Montepulciano

Waitress in the Piazza Grande

Chiusi flag

The magnificent Renaissance church of San Biagio, designed by Antonio Sangallo the Elder, lies at the end of an avenue of cypresses welcoming visitors to **Montepulciano** (pop. 14,000), birthplace of the Renaissance poet and humanist Politian (1454–94), and one of the major tourist centres of Tuscany. This town, also known as the 'pearl of the 16th century', has several magnificent Renaissance palazzi and also some marvellous wine. The celebrated *Vino Nobile di Montepulciano* needs to mature in oak casks for a minimum of two years before earning its DOCG label. A dry wine with an unmistakably noble taste, it is considered by many to be the king of Italian reds. The nicest wine cellar in town is probably the 'Cantina del Redi'; its underground rooms were built by Antonio da Sangallo the Elder in the 15th century.

The Palazzo Comunale in the Piazza Grande is reminiscent of the Palazzo Vecchio – and not without reason, because Montepulciano was ruled by Florence from the end of the 14th century onwards. The Duomo contains a magnificent ★ **triptych** by Taddeo di Bartolo; and the three-storeyed Renaissance Palazzo Cantucci has a cellar full of even more *Nobile*.

Continue now across the scenic hilly landscape with its marvellous views to the medieval town of Chianciano and its newer section, **Chianciano Terme** (pop. 7,200). This town has over 250 hotels, and is one of the most famous spa resorts in Italy. The local advertising slogan pronounces: *Chianciàno – fegato sàno* ('Chianciano means a healthy liver').

The Etruscans chose the strategically favourable location on the hilltop between the Tiber and Arno valleys for the mightiest of their cities, **Chiusi** (pop. 9,000). The plateau of calcareous tufa upon which the town stands is surrounded by olive groves and vineyards, and it was from up here that the Etruscans ruled over large regions of Latium under their legendary leader Lars Porsenna.

At the beginning of the 3rd century BC, Chiusi was taken by the Romans. During the Middle Ages the town became increasingly insignificant, and the unhealthy marshes nearby ushered in decline and malaria. It was only when the Canale Maestro, connecting the swamps of the Chiana with the Arno, was built during the 18th century that the region was finally drained. The two romantic lakes here, the Lago di Montepulciano and the Lago di Chiusi, are all that remain today of the former marshland.

Before visiting the Etruscan sights, take a quick look at the Duomo, which was founded in the 6th century. The beautiful columns in the three-aisled interior were taken from Roman buildings; the strange, mosaic-like painting dates from 1887. From the Cathedral Museum (Museo della Cattedrale: daily 9.30am–12.45pm, Sunday and public holidays also 3–6pm), which is definitely worth a visit, it's possible to walk along a long gallery, part of the labyrinth of underground passageways dating from Etruscan times.

The Duomo is 6th-century

The ★ **Museo Nazionale Etrusco** (Monday to Saturday 9am–2pm, Sunday 9am–1pm) is famous for its collection of cinerary urns, and the exhibits also include reliefs, sculptures, black-figure Attic vases and sarcophagi.

Mosaic from the Museo Nazionale Etrusco

75

Chiusi's enormous ★ **Etruscan necropolis**, which surrounds the whole town, is unique. A guide from the museum accompanies visitors to the tombs that are open; unlike many other tombs in Tuscany, these ones still contain several paintings, urns and sarcophagi.

Traces of the Etruscans

Drive around Monte Cetona (1,148m/3,766ft) and via the small medieval town of Sarteano towards Radicofani; the road is full of bends and has some great views along it. Soon the town of ★ **Radicofani** (783m/2,568ft above sea-level, pop. 1,300) comes into view. It's hard to miss: this town was a fortress that was repeatedly fought over. The Sienese got the upper hand in the 15th century, and in 1559 Radicofani was the last Sienese castle to surrender to Florence – it decided to do so only after hearing of the fall of Montalcino.

The very beautiful Romanesque church of San Pietro is worth visiting for the valuable Della Robbia terracottas inside; there's also a very good *Madonna and Child with Saints* altarpiece by Andrea della Robbia in the church of Sant'Agata opposite.

The enormous former volcano known as **Monte Amiata** (1,738m/5,702ft) rises very suddenly from the hilly country surrounding it. The various zones of vegetation on its slopes range from cornfields, vineyards and

A homely atmosphere

olive groves to thick forests of chestnut and beech. A well-surfaced road leads to the summit, one of the most popular skiing regions in Tuscany during the winter, and the ★ **view** from the top often extends as far as Elba, Corsica, Siena and Orvieto.

Monte Amiata is at its most attractive in the autumn, when the whole mountain is a mass of colour. The marked routes for 'Amiata Trekking' cover the various zones very accurately; the 28km (17 miles) of footpaths here lie at altitudes of between 1,050m (3,444ft) and 1,250m (4,101ft). A trip around the mountain by car travelling through the various medieval towns on its slopes, with all the views across the hilly Tuscan countryside, is also a rewarding experience. Three of these mountains towns definitely merit closer inspection: Abbadia San Salvatore, Santa Fiora and Arcidisso.

Abbadia San Salvatore (pop. 7,200) was named after the Benedictine ★ **Abbey of San Salvatore**, founded in the year 743 by the Lombard king Ratchis on the spot where he saw a vision. The story of his mystical experience is related in the baroque frescoes in the chapel to the right of the presbytery. The abbey church here today was begun in 1036, and its narrow facade still bears many Romanesque features. The most fascinating part of the building, however, is the 8th-century ★ **crypt**, which dates from a previous structure on the site. The 36 columns with their elaborately-carved capitals are the best-preserved Lombard structure in Tuscany.

The medieval part of the town, the ★ **Borgo**, looks especially weird and mysterious when a thick fog descends – quite a common occurrence on Monte Amiata.

The autumn landscape

Santa Fiora (pop. 3,000) is a very picturesque village. Its Romanesque Pieve di SS Fiora e Lucilla contains a unique collection of works by Andrea Della Robbia and his workshop. Several details, among them the sleeping soldiers in the Resurrection scene, are brilliantly executed and worth stopping off for.

Completing the picture

Arcidosso (pop. 4,100) is dominated by a massive castle, built during the Middle Ages by the Aldobrandeschi family, who used to rule a large part of the region between Amiata and the sea. The highlight here isn't so much the medieval town as the Parco Faunistico dell'Amiata (Monte Amiata Wildlife Park). The moufflons, deer and chamois in the first three compounds may not be all that much of a rarity, but the wolves in the fourth one definitely are. Several well-marked hiking routes lead across the park to the various sections.

The next three towns on this route – Sorano, Sovana and Pitigliano – are three southern Tuscan jewels. The roads, hewn out of the hills by the Etruscans, are an experience in themselves (eg the stretch between Sovana and Pitigliano). The calcareous tufa retains a lot of water, and the thick, evergreen vegetation, with its ferns and ivy, is almost jungle-like.

More fine wines

The small medieval town of **Sorano** (pop. 4,200) has an Orsini fortress and several charming narrow streets in its old town. There are numerous Etruscan rock tombs along the road between Sorano and Sovana, and approaching the town from this direction is genuinely spectacular.

The village of **Sovan**a lies on a ridge overlooking a broad panorama. It's barely more than a single street, which widens at the centre to form a piazza. Sovana's magnificent Romanesque ★ **Cathedral**, which contains some very fine capitals, stands at the end of the village, as does the birthplace of Hildebrand of Sovana (who later became Pope Gregory VII).

There are several interesting Etruscan necropoli nearby, most of them rock tombs of the 2nd century BC. The largest tomb, the **tomba di Ildebrando**, was of course named after Hildebrand; the monumental grave is decorated with pillars, capitals and steps.

The town of **Pitigliano** (pop. 4,300) should definitely be viewed from the church of Madonna delle Grazie; the town's unique skyline can be seen to its best advantage from here. The magnificent Palazzo Orsini and the narrow medieval streets in the old part of the town, built above Etruscan caves, cellars and tombs, lend the place a very special atmosphere. The wine, Bianco di Pitigliano, is also very fine. Albinia and the sea can be reached from Pitigliano via the N74.

Art History

Opposite: Botticelli's Birth of Venus

The Beginnings

The oldest surviving cultural artefacts in Tuscany were produced by settlers in the Lunigiana around 4,000 years ago. The exact function of these *statue-stelae* (primitive menhirs) is unclear, but they can still be admired at the museum in Pontremoli (*see page 59*).

The Etruscans

An Etruscan smile

The art of the Etruscans is much more approachable. The dead on the early funerary urns have fixed smiles, like their Greek counterparts, but from the 4th and 5th centuries BC they start growing more realistic. Some of the Etruscans in the museum in Chiusi are even quite ugly. A complex cult of the dead led to the construction of enormous necropoli. The dead were buried along with everything they had owned in life: weapons, jewellery, jars. The most important archaeological museums are in Florence, Volterra, Arezzo and Chiusi, and the finest burial mounds can be seen at Populonia, Vetulonia and Chiusi; in Roselle (*see page 66*) there's a whole city to visit.

79

The Romans

The Romans built several amphitheatres in Tuscany, such as those in Fiesole, Roselle, Volterra and Arezzo. Their art can be admired in archaeological museums – and also in churches. Capitals, pillars, marble slabs (even with inscriptions) and sarcophagi were re-used to build new structures. Art historians refer to this practice as 'spoliation' – 'recycling' would be the more every-day term. Roman basilicas were used for judicial and commercial purposes, and were large oblong halls with double colonnades and a semicircular apse – this ground-plan was borrowed by the Early Christians for the design of their first chapels and churches.

Volterra amphitheatre

The Romanesque Period

San Miniato al Monte in Florence

Numerous rural churches in Tuscany retain the basic basilica shape. Their simplicity is as fascinating as the mythological and fabulous creatures – sea-serpents, monsters, dragons – carved into their capitals and reliefs.

Of course the ambitious Tuscan towns were not satisfied with these simple structures. Pisa built itself a magnificent Romanesque cathedral – not only for the glory of God but also as an expression of civic pride. The same applies to the church of San Michele in Foro in Lucca, and the Baptistery and church of San Miniato al Monte in Florence. The latter two buildings possess a grandiose harmony only otherwise equalled by the Collegiata San Andrea in Empoli.

The sculptor Nicola Pisano (1220–78) was active during the Late Romanesque period. His chancels in the baptistery in Pisa and in Siena cathedral mark the transition to the Gothic style which his son Giovanni (1245–1314) adopted and developed further in his reliefs on the pulpits in Pisa cathedral and in Sant'Andrea in Pistoia. The work of Giovanni Pisano reflects not only Gothic grace, however; antiquity can be felt far more clearly in his work than in his father's. Artists were becoming individual personalities, and were no longer anonymous 'craftsmen'; the Museo Medievale e Moderno in Arezzo contains a work by Margaritone which is thought to be the oldest-known signed painting in Italy.

The Gothic Period

The Gothic style was imported into Italy by Cistercian monks from France. It became popular in the monasteries of the various orders in the 13th century: the Franciscans, Dominicans and Augustinians. Broad naves and rows of chapels in the transepts are distinctive features of the architecture in mendicant order buildings: the pointed windows are there, but the 'soaring' quality familiar from the French cathedrals is absent. These broad churches were based around the new idea of preaching to the congregation. Even the walls were used for this purpose: the frescoes we see today were an effective visual means of familiarising people with Christian themes. Painting now assumed great importance: it was no longer *al secco* but *al fresco*, ie painted on to damp plaster.

The Byzantine heritage, clearly visible in the painted wooden crosses with their rigid figures and stylised facial *Giotto fresco* expressions, was superseded by the Gothic style in Siena.

Artists such as Duccio (1255–1319), Simone Martini (1284–1344), Pietro (1280–1345) and Ambrogio Lorenzetti (1290–1348) are particularly famous.

In Florence it was the new spirituality of Giotto (1266–1337) that pointed the way from the Gothic to the Renaissance style. His figures are physically at ease with themselves, much of the former the stiffness is gone. The fascinating architectural motifs in Giotto's work and the interplay of light and shadow combine to form a new and penetrating harmony.

The Renaissance

One of the most important artists of the Renaissance was Brunelleschi (1377–1446). His perfectly-planned structures and his use of space are based on antique models, and his masterpiece is perhaps the Pazzi Chapel in Santa Croce. The rediscovery of geometrical perspective was a real revolution, and paintings suddenly gained depth.

Tribute Money by Masaccio
Donatello's David

Masaccio (1401–28) put this technique to good use in his fresco of the Trinity in Santa Maria Novella in Florence, and also in the Brancacci Chapel in Santa Maria del Carmine. Benozzo Gozzoli (1420–98) started telling colourful stories in paint (Palazzo Medici-Riccardi); Ghirlandaio (1449–94) did portraits of wealthy members of the circle around Lorenzo the Magnificent (Santa Trinità), and Botticelli's *Spring* (Uffizi Gallery) is still enchants today. *David* (Bargello) by Donatello (1386–1466) represents the first sculpture of a naked human being since antiquity and much of the later 15th-century painting in Florence stems from his influence.

81

Many other artists achieved immortality through their work: Ghiberti (1348–1455), with his baptistery doors in Florence; Luca della Robbia (1399–1482) with his outdoor pulpit in Prato (Cathedral Museum); or the Sienese artist Jacopo della Quercia (1367–1438) with his *Ilaria* (in the cathedral). Another all-round genius in Siena was Francesco di Giorgio Martini (1439–1502), an architect, painter and inventor.

Michelangelo's Doni Holy Family

The Renaissance in Florence entered its peak phase with the advent of Leonardo da Vinci (1452–1519) and Michelangelo (1475–1564), and declined very soon afterwards: Michelangelo left for Rome with Raphael (1483–1520) to work for Pope Julius II. Economic and political decay in Florence – and Tuscany as a whole – had a negative effect. The major families could no longer afford to make commissions, and there was no longer any kind of independent art scene. The only family to build anything were the Medici, who continued to glorify themselves rather than humanity in general. Giambologna (1529–1608), who came from Flanders, was the first foreign artist to be successful in Florence.

Festivals & Folklore

Flag bearer in Siena

Calcio Storico

Palio delle Contrade, Siena: This famous horse-race around Siena's central square, the *Campo*, is held on **2 July** and **16 August** each year; 10 of the 17 sections of the city known as the *contrade* take part in each race respectively. The event begins with a colourful procession in 14th-century historical costume, followed by the victory celebration. The Palio is far from being a tourist attraction; it has great ritual significance for the Sienese.

Giostra del Saracino, Arezzo: **The Saracen Tournament**, a historic jousting match, takes place on Arezzo's Piazza Grande on the fourth Sunday in June and the first Sunday in September. Each of the four quarters of the city enters two 'knights' armed with lances to fight the Saracen (a large, rotating wooden puppet).

Gioco del Ponte, Pisa: This sham fight between the people living on opposite sides of the Arno takes place on the last Sunday in June, on the Ponte di Mezzo. After a colourful procession, the combatants use contraptions on rails in an attempt to take the bridge. The 'Gioco del Ponte' is the high point of 'Giugno Pisano', which also includes a regatta and the 'Festa di San Ranieri', preceded on the night before by a candlelight festival on the banks of the Arno to commemorate the city's patron saint.

Calcio Storico, Florence: This historic football match, held on the Piazza Santa Croce, takes place three times in June (always on **24 June**, the day of the city's patron saint, John the Baptist). It commemorates a similar match played by soldiers trapped in the city in 1530.

Scoppio del Carro, Florence: On **Easter Sunday** a cart *(carro)* decorated with flowers and loaded with fireworks is set up in front of the baptistery. A mechanical dove swoops out of the cathedral door and into the cart; if the fireworks ignite, it bodes a good year.

Sacred Girdle of the Virgin, Prato: At Easter, on **1 May**, **15 August**, **8 September** and at Christmas the Sacred Girdle of the Virgin Mary is placed on show in the outer pulpit of the cathedral. Members of the city council attend the ceremony dressed in historical costume.

Giostra dell'Orso, Pistoia: After a magnificent procession held on **25 July** every year, 12 knights take part in a medieval jousting tournament; the aim is to hit two stylised bears with their lances to the sound of drum rolls and fanfares. The bear *(orso)* is the heraldic animal of Pistoia, and the Giostra is the highlight of the town's 'Luglio Pistoiese' festival.

Palio dei Balestrieri, Sansepolcro: In May the crossbowmen of Sansepolcro travel to Gubbio (Umbria) for a contest. On the second Sunday in September the crossbowmen of Gubbio return the visit.

Besides these traditional festivals, there are also many annual cultural events:

Florence – second Sunday each month: antiques market on Piazza Santo Spirito; May and June: Maggio musicale fiorentino; **7 September**: Rificolona lantern festival on Piazza SS Annunziata.

Fiesole – July to August: Estate Fiesolana, with concerts, films, opera and ballet.

Pisa – Wednesday and Saturday: market in the Via S Francesco; every second weekend (except July/August): antiques fair on Ponte di Mezzo.

Siena – every Wednesday: market in the Piazza La Lizza; mid-August: Siena music festival, with concerts and summer courses.

Lucca – third weekend of every month: antiques market outside the Duomo, and artists' fair on Piazza dell' Arancio; first weekend of every month: crafts fair on Piazza San Giusto; weekends in March: camellia exhibitions in local towns; April to June: 'Sagra Musicale Lucchese' religious music festival; September: 'Settembre Lucchese' wine and olive-oil market on Piazza San Michele in Foro with cultural events; **13 September**: candlelight procession in honour of the 'Volto Santo' *(see page 38)*.

Trading antiques in Lucca

Arezzo – every Saturday: market on the Piazza Sant' Agostino; first weekend of every month: largest antiques fair in Tuscany on the Piazza Grande; August: International Polyphony Festival in honour of Guido d'Arezzo, who invented musical notation in the 11th century.

Local arts and crafts

Prato – the 'Prato Estate' festival in the summer has lots of concerts, and there's an open-air cinema too.

Pistoia – second weekend of every month (except July/ August): antiques fair in the Piazza Duomo; early July: 'Luglio Pistoiese', with cultural and musical events; end of July until early September: concerts in villas and medieval provincial towns (contact APT for further details).

San Miniato al Tedesco – every second Sunday in the month, except August: largest ecological market in Tuscany, organic wines, olive oil, honey; every first Sunday in the month, except August: antiques fair; third Sunday in October: truffle and mushroom festival; November: 'Novembre Sanminiatese', music, culture, truffle-eating.

Volterra – March to June: 'Primavera Musicale Volterrana', Saturday concerts in the Palazzo dei Priori.

Massa Marittima – **20 May** and second Sunday in August: historical flag-waving festival and crossbow tournament; July to August: antiques market.

Pienza – first Sunday in September: 'Fiera del Cacio' cheese market.

Montepulciano – July until first week in August: 'Cantiere internazionale d'Arte'; last Sunday in August: 'Bravio', uphill barrel-rolling contest, historical procession.

Food and Drink

Opposite: a prospect to savour

The basis of Tuscan cooking is olive oil. It's not just any old oil, but the famous *Olio d'Oliva Extra Vergine* – and the smell alone is superb. Its colour ranges from golden yellow to greenish. The washed olives are pressed mechanically, and then the oil is filtered and freed of sediment. Any chemical manipulation is strictly forbidden.

The oil is accompanied by all kinds of fresh herbs, including sage, thyme, basil, parsley and also garlic and onions. Tuscans like their food to be simple yet substantial: a toasted piece of fresh garlic bread drenched in olive oil (*fettunta*), for instance, a barley soup (*farro*), a delicious slice of charcoal-grilled T-bone or rib steak (*bistecca alla fiorentina*), or a bowl of lamb's lettuce (*rucola*).

The basis of Tuscan cooking

Meals generally begin with typically Tuscan hors d'oeuvres (*antipasti*), such as *crostini* (toasted bread with liver sausage) or *fettunta* (*see above*). Tuscan salami is also a treat for the taste buds; a good variety is *finocchiona* (with fennel seeds). One of the most popular types of sausage is made with wild boar called *salsiccie di cinghiale*. Another excellent starter or side-dish is *pinzimonio*, raw vegetables dipped in a salted and spiced olive-oil sauce.

Simple but substantial food

85

Tuscany's soups make delicious hot starters (*primi piatti*); they include *ribollita* (vegetable, cabbage and bread with a dash of olive oil), and also *pasta e fagioli* (pasta and bean stew). The noodle dish par excellence in Tuscany is *pappardelle*, with hare sauce (*sugo di lepre*); a wise choice on hot days is also *panzanella*, a cold dish made up of bread, tomatoes, fresh vegetables, olive oil and basil.

Vegetarians sometimes have a difficult time in Tuscany; two possible choices, however, are *tortino di carciofi* (baked artichoke prepared with beaten egg and aromatic herbs) and *funghi alla griglia* (grilled mushrooms).

The *bistecca alla fiorentina*, a huge slab of beef grilled over hot charcoal and seasoned with finest olive oil, salt and pepper is superb; game such as hare (*lepre*), wild boar (*cinghiale*) and pheasant (*fagiano*) often appears in stews (*in umido*). Tuscans also love tripe, though *trippa alla fiorentina* (tripe cooked in tomato sauce with Parmesan cheese) may not be to everyone's taste. Those eager to experiment, however, can also try *cervella* (brains), *lampredotto* (cow intestine) and *granelli* (testicles).

Fresh produce

Fish and seafood of all kinds are available along the coast: *cacciuccio alla livornese*, a mixture of red mullet, crab and squid with a tomato, onion, garlic and *Chianti* sauce topped with croutons, is particularly tasty.

Alongside the typical Italian side-dishes (*contorni*) such as chips (*patate fritte*), salad (*insalata*) or cooked vegetables (*verdura cotta*), the Tuscans also make the delicious *fagioli all'uccelletto* (white beans in tomato sauce).

A treat for the taste buds

A selection of top brands

Many bars sell snacks as well

One particularly good cheese is *pecorino* (ewe's cheese) from the south of the region. And for pudding (*dolci*) there are some very fine cakes to choose from, eg *Torta con i bischeri* (pine-nut cake), or *cantuccini* (almond-flavoured biscuits) which are usually dunked in *vin santo*, the typical Tuscan dessert wine.

Mineral water (*acqua minerale*) can be drunk either fizzy (*gasata*) or still (*naturale*), but the main beverage is wine.

The most famous Tuscan wine is *Chianti*, from the region of the same name south of Florence; the various different varieties, which are also grown on the hills around Arezzo, Siena and Pisa, are all ruby-red in colour and have a relatively high alcohol content of between 11 and 13 percent. *Chianti Classico*, from the classic wine area between Florence and Siena, can be recognised by the distinctive black cockerel (*gallo nero*) on the label.

But Tuscany produces a whole series of other top wines apart from *Chianti*. *Brunello di Montalcino* is one of the best reds in the world, and is produced in the area around Montalcino to the south of Siena; another excellent wine comes from the same area, the famous *Vino nobile di Montepulciano*.

As for whites, one of the most well-known is *Vernaccia* from San Gimignano, which goes well with fish dishes. *Galestro* is a newer, lighter table wine; its light-yellow flaxen colour is very summery, and its relatively low alcohol content (10.5 percent) makes it ideal for drinking on warm evenings outdoors.

One of the specialities of Tuscany is the dessert wine known as *vin santo*. Its taste is reminiscent of sherry, and it takes three to four years to mature properly. *Vin santo* also makes a delicious apéritif, and is often accompanied by *cantuccini* (almond-flavoured biscuits).

Snacks

Two popular Tuscan snacks for in between meals are *focaccine* (a flat roll with salami, ham or cheese) and *cecina*, a flat pizza made of chick-pea flour. Those with a sweet tooth should try the following sticky roadside specials: *fritelle, frati* or *bomboloni*.

Restaurants and Menus

When in Italy, note that pasta dishes are regarded as hors d'oeuvres, and can often only be ordered along with a main course (*secondo piatto*). The waiters don't add up the bills separately either, but produce one for the whole table. There's usually an extra cover charge for bread (*pane e coperto*), costing between L1,000 and L3,000 per person.

Tourist menus generally cost between L10,000 and L15,000; this price includes a cover charge (*coperto*) and service (*servizio*). A meal à la carte will cost over L15,000, and in good restaurants at least L30,000. Service in restaurants is sometimes not included either (10–15 percent). Typical Tuscan cuisine can be enjoyed quite cheaply at 'Agriturismo' country inns.

The restaurants listed below are suggestions from some of Tuscany's most popular destinations, listed alphabetically. They are divided into three categories: $$$ = expensive; $$ = medium-priced; $ = cheap.

Arezzo: **$$Le Tastevin**, Via de'Cenci 9, typical Tuscan food, piano bar; **$$Bucadi San Francesco**, Piazza San Francesco 1, famous cellar restaurant; **$La Lancia d'Oro**, Piazza Grande, good Arezzo cuisine.

Colle di Val d'Elsa: **$$$Arnolfo**, Piazza S Caterina 1, first-class establishment; **$$$L'Antica Trattoria**, Piazza Arnolfo 23, superb gourmet cuisine.

Cortona: **$$Loggetta**, Piazza Pescheria 3, Tuscan cuisine in basement of 16th-century palazzo; **$La Grotta**, Piazza Baldelli 3, small family-run establishment.

Fiesole: **$Il Lordo**, Piazza Mina di Fiesole.

Florence: **$$$Enoteca Pinchiorri**, Via Ghibellina 87, best gourmet restaurant in the city; **$$$Loggia**, Piazzale Michelangelo 1, superb cuisine, with view of Florence; **$$Mamma Gina**, Borgo San Jacopo 37r, Tuscan cuisine in 15th-century palazzo; **$$Acquerello**, Via Ghibellina 156r, serves food till very late; **$Il Latini**, Via Palchetti 6, rustic Tuscan cuisine; **$Il Cibreo**, Piazza Ghiberti 35, pleasant osteria with delicatessen attached.

87

Unpretentious cuisine

Cordial staff

Livorno: **$$Ara Gosta**, Piazza dell'Arsenale 6, famous for its *cacciuccio* fish soup; **$$La Barcarola**, Viale Carducci 63, good seafood.

Lucca: **$$Buca di Sant'Antonio**, Via della Cervia 1/3, excellent cooking; **$$Antico Caffè delle Mura**, Piazzale Vittorio Emanuele 2, historic café on the city wall; **$Da Giulio**, Via delle Conce 45, typical cuisine of western Tuscany.

Massa Marittima: **$$Taverna del Vecchio Borgo**, Via Parenti 12, typical Maremma cuisine.

Montalcino: **$Trattoria Sciame**, Via Ricasoli 9, good home cooking, Tuscan sausage specialities.

Montepulciano: **$Il Cantuccio**, Via delle Cantine, *pici* and grilled meat; **$Diva**, Via Gracciano 92, simple food, *pici* and lamb.

Pescia: **$$Cecco**, Piazza Mazzini 95, excellent local cuisine.

Ubiquitous pasta

Pienza: **$Buca delle fate**, Corse Rossellino 38a, simple but excellent cuisine, in 16th-century Palazzo Gonzaga.

Pisa: **$$$$Sergio**, Lungarno Pacinotti 1, one of the top restaurants in Tuscany; **$$Bruno**, Via Luigi Bianchi 12, Pisan cuisine; **$La Cereria**, Via Gori 33, restaurant-pizzeria with pleasant inner courtyard.

Pistoia: **$$Leon Rosso**, Via Panciatichi 4, good Tuscan cuisine; **$Rafanelli**, Via Agostino, Tuscan home cooking.

Eat inside or outside

Prato: **$$Tonio**, Piazza Mercatale 161, good local cuisine.

San Gimignano: **$$Griglia**, Via S Matteo 14, grill specialities, magnificent viewing terrace; **$$Stella**, Via S Matteo 77, very good Tuscan cuisine.

San Miniato al Tedesco: **$$Canapone**, Piazza Buonaparte 5, typical Tuscan cuisine, truffles when in season.

Siena: **$$Mangia**, Piazza del Campo 42, Tuscan cuisine on the Campo; **$$Osteria Le Logge**, Via del Porrione 33, Sienese cuisine; **$Papei**, Piazza del Mercato 6, typical trattoria.

Volterra: **$$Etruria**, Piazza dei Priori 6/8, game specialities in an old palazzo on the central square; **$Beppino**, Via delle Prigioni 15/19, good Tuscan home cooking.

Sports

Tuscany is the ideal place to combine a cultural holiday with all kinds of sporting activities, by the sea or up in the mountains.

Swimming

Plenty of flat, sandy beaches

The sandy beaches of the Versilia in the north alternate with the rocky bays of the Etruscan Riviera until everything gradually levels out into the flat sandy beaches of the Maremma in the south. River estuaries are best avoided, because of possible pollution.

Sailing

There are sailing schools in Viareggio, Marina di Pietrasanta (information from APT, *see page 96*) and also in Vada (circolo Velico Pietrabianca, tel: 0586-788302).

Learn to sail

Diving

The main diving schools can be found at Forte dei Marmi, Viareggio (information from APT, *see page 96*), Porto Santo Stefano (tel: 0564-937098), and Porto Ercole (tel: 0564-810145).

89

Motor boats

There are motor-boat clubs at Cecina, Marina di Carrara, Marina di Massa and at Viareggio.

Fishing

A prize catch

Fishing in the ocean and underwater is allowed; no permit is required. Anglers wishing to fish inland need permission from the respective local administrative body. Foreign tourists can often obtain special permits quite cheaply that are valid for up to six months. For further details contact the **Federazione Italiana della Pesca Sportiva**, Viale Tiziano 70, Roma.

Hiking

Hiking, or 'trekking' as the Italians call it, is becoming very fashionable. The long-distance tour known as Grande Escursione Appenninica (or GEA for short) takes 25 days and covers a distance of 400km (250 miles) through the Tuscan Apennines. The individual sections are described in the *Grandi Itinerari in Toscana* series published by Tamari.

Further information about the suggested routes can be obtained from the APTs (see page 96) or from the **Club Alpino Italiano**, Via Studio 5, Florence, who also organise excursions (open Monday to Saturday 6–7.30pm). The bookshop **'Il Viaggio'**, Borgo degli Albizzi 4/r, Florence, sells good maps and guides for hikers.

Cycling

This is also becoming extremely popular. The APTs will provide information on cycle hire and touring routes. Bicycles are allowed on board local trains (*treni regionali*), and an environmentally-friendly variation is *Treni e Bici* (train and bike) with combined tours in the Garfagnana.

Riding

There are riding stables (*maneggi*) all over Tuscany. Information can be obtained from all APTs, but one very well-organised company is Garfagnana Turismo Equestre (GTE) which does rides through the Garfagnana that can last up to several days (**Azienda Agrituristica La Garfagnana**, Castiglio Garfagnana, tel: 0583-68705). Another good tip is **Garfagnana Vacanze**, Piazza delle Erbe 1, Castelnuovo Garfagnana, tel: 0583-65169; they're specialists for outdoor holidays in the Apuan Alps (hiking, mountain-biking or riding).

Golf

There are several courses in Tuscany, including the majestically situated Ugolino course near Florence, and others at Punta Ala, Viareggio and Tirrenia (Pisa).

Gliding

See Tuscany from the air

This is available in Lucca, Siena and in Borgo San Lorenzo. Contact the **Centreo Nazionale di Volo a Vela dell'Aereo Club d'Italia**, Via Rosatelli 111, Rieti, tel: 0746-202138.

Spa resorts

There are health spas practically everywhere. For further details, the ENIT does a brochure available in English. The major spas include Chianciano Terme, Sarteano, Montecatini Terme, Monsummano Terme, Bagni di Lucca, San Giuliano Terme, San Carlo sopra Massa, Equi Terme, Rapollano Terme and Saturnia.

Montecatini Terme

Skiing

There is skiing near Abetone, Cutigliano and Maresca in the Pistoian Apennines with 50km (31 miles) of piste and over 30 lifts, and also at Monte Amiata (ski school, 10 lifts). For details, contact **APT** Abetone Pistoia Montagna Pistoiese, Via G Marconi 16, 51028 San Marcello Pistoiese, tel: 0573-63 01 45, fax: 62 21 20; **APT** Via Mentana 97, 53021 Abbadia San Salvatore, tel: 0577-77 86 08, fax: 77 90 13.

Horse racing

There are major race meetings in Florence, Montecatini, Pisa, Livorno and Grosseto.

Other Activities

Italian courses

Several language schools do courses for foreigners. For further information contact the ENIT and the APTs. Note: university courses tend to be cheaper (**Centro di Cultura per Stranieri**, Via Vittorio Emanuele II 64, Florence; Via Banchi di Sotto 55, Siena; Via Santa Maria 36, Pisa).

Music courses

These are held at the **Accademia Musicale Chigiana**, Via di Città 89, Siena. **Musica Viva** offers a range of courses in choral, instrumental and chamber music, also for families, combining nicely with the dolce vita of Tuscany.

Farm holidays

Agriturismo (*see Accommodation*, page 100) is the Italian term for good-value farm holidays, which often include wine-tasting, sports facilities and chances to sample traditional cookery. The **Agriturist** headquarters in Tuscany is at Piazza San Firenze 3, Florence, tel: 055-287838.

Art courses

Several institutions in Florence hold courses on art techniques or art history. The **Università dell'Arte**, Villa II Ventaglio, Via delle Forbici 24/26, tel: 055-570216, and the **British Institute**, Palazzo Lanfredini, Lugarno Guicciardini 9, tel: 284 4031, hold specialised art appreciation courses. The **Instituto d'Arte di Firenze**, Via dell'Alloro, tel: 055-283142, has practical courses in painting, design, sculpture, ceramics and jewellery-making.

Landscape for artists

Getting There

By air

Apart from the airport at Pisa, there is the international airport of Peretola (also known as Amerigo Vespucci Airport), serving Florence. Flights to Peretola tend to be more expensive. Pisa is served by several charter companies (eg Italy Sky Shuttle) in addition to scheduled flights (eg Alitalia, Air France, Lufthansa, British Airways and Ryan Air); Peretola mainly serves business travellers. Meridiana flies to Florence from London Gatwick. Cheaper flights to Bologna and Rome are also worth considering.

There are no direct flights between North America and Tuscany. However, TWA and Air Canada are among the North American carriers who operate flights to Milan and Rome. With good onward train connections, this is a good option for visitors from the US.

For further information in the UK, contact: **Italy Sky Shuttle**, tel: 0181-748 1333/4999; fax 0181-748 6381.
Alitalia (Florence office), tel: 055-27888.
Alitalia (Pisa office), tel: 050-501570.
British Airways (Florence office), tel: 055-218655.
British Airways (Pisa Office), tel: 050-501838.
TWA (Florence office), tel: 055-230 69 -56.
Airport information, Florence Peretola (Amerigo Vespucci Airport), tel: 055-373498.
Airport information, Pisa (Galileo Galilei Airport), tel: 050-500707.

93

By road

Italy's toll motorways are connected to those of Northern Europe via Brenner and Tarvisio (Austria) and Chiasso (Switzerland). Be prepared for long queues at weekends and during peak holiday periods in the area of Milan, Florence and Bologna.

By rail

Tickets for Italian railways are issued by the **Italian State Railways**, CIT, Marco Polo House, 3–5 Lansdowne Road, Croydon, Surrey, tel: 0181-686 0677/5533. In the US, contact CIT, 666 Fifth Avenue, New York, NY 10103, tel: 800-223 0230. In Canada, contact CIT, 1450 City Counsellers, Suite 750, Montreal, Quebec H3A 2E6, tel: (514) 845 9101.

The Tuscan provincial capitals of Massa, Pisa, Livorno and Grosseto are on the main railway line from Milan to Rome; Florence and Arezzo lie on the second important route between Bologna and Rome. There are connections from Florence or Pisa to Prato, Pistoia, Lucca and Siena. Children pay half the fare in Italy. More information on special offers from DER and CIT travel agencies.

Road signs can be confusing

All the major towns have efficient bus services

Heed the road signs

Getting Around

By bus

There are efficient bus networks in all the major towns and cities in Tuscany, and connections across country to smaller towns and villages too. The most important bus lines are: LAZZI, SITA (in Florence, near the railway station), TRAIN (in Siena, Piazza San Domenico), COPIT (in Pistoia, near the church of San Francesco), ATAM (Arezzo, station square) and CLAP (Lucca, Piazza Verdi, near the information centre).

By car

Most historic cities have introduced partial or complete bans on cars in the city centre. Cars should be left in the car parks outside the cities and then public transport taken.

The state highways in Tuscany are the No 1 'Aurelia', west of Pisa, and national motorways (*autostrade*), the A11 'Firenze-Mare' and the A12 'Sestri Levante-Livorno'. Tolls on the motorways are expensive.

By train

The state-subsidised rail network is a relatively cheap and convenient form of transport for travelling between major cities in Tuscany. The main Rome-Milan line is convenient for Bologna, Florence and Arezzo, while the Rome-Genoa line serves Pisa, Livorno and Grosseto. The Florence-Siena route is much faster by coach. Pisa Centrale serves Pisa city, while Pisa Aeroporto serves the airport. In Florence, Santa Maria Novella is the main station for the city, Rifredi is the station served by the high-speed *Pendolino* train. Reservations are mandatory for superior trains (*Pendolino*, Eurocity and Intercity services) and tickets should be purchased in advance.

Facts for the Visitor

Travel documents

Visitors from European Union countries require either a passport or identification card to enter Italy. Holders of passports from most other countries do not require visas for a period not exceeding three months.

Customs

There have been practically no customs limits for nationals of EU member states since 1993. The following are just rough guidelines: 800 cigarettes, 200 cigars, 1kg of tobacco, 90 litres of wine.

Currency regulations

Unlimited amounts of foreign currency and Italian lire may be brought in and out of Italy, but need to be declared if the sum exceeds L20 million.

Tourist information

Here are the addresses of the Italian Tourist Office (ENIT):
UK: 1 Princes Street, London W1, tel: 0171-408 1254.
US: 630 Fifth Avenue, Suite 1565, New York NY 10111, tel: (212) 245-4822.

The national flag

When in Italy, contact the APT (Azienda di Promozione Turistica). They'll help with finding hotels, organising farm holidays, renting bikes, etc. They also have city plans and lists of the opening times of museums and exhibitions.

Call in at the local tourist office

Florence: APT, Via Manzoni 16, 50121 Firenze, tel: 055-23320, fax: 234 6285; Piazza Stazione, tel: 212245; Chiasso Baroncelli 17r (Piazza Signoria), tel: 230 2124; Via Cavour 1r, tel: 2 0832.

Fiesole: APT, Piazza Mino da Fiesole 35, 50014 Fiesole, tel: 055-598720, fax: 598822.

Pisa: APT, Via Benedetto Croce 26, 56100 Pisa, tel: 050-40096, fax: 40903; Piazza della Stazione tel: 42291; Piazza del Duomo tel: 560464.

Siena: APT, Via di Città 43, 53100 Siena, tel: 0577-42209, fax: 28 10 41; Piazza del Campo tel: 280551, fax: 270676.

Lucca: APT, Piazza Guidiccioni 2, 55100 Lucca, tel: 0583-49 12 05, fax: 49 07 66; Vecchia Porta San Donato, Piazzale Verdi, tel/fax: 419689.

Arezzo: APT, Piazza Risorgimento 116, 52100 Arezzo, tel: 0575-23952, fax: 28042; Piazza della Repubblica 28, tel: 377678.

Cortona: APT, Via Nazionale 72, 52044 Cortona, tel/fax: 0575-630352.

Prato: APT, Via Cairoli 48/52, 50047 Prato, tel: 0574-24112.

Heaps of information at hand

Pistoia: APT, Via Roma 1 (in the Palazzo dei Vescovi), 51100 Pistoia, tel: 0573-21622, fax: 34327.

Montecatini Terme: APT, Viale Verdi 56, Montecatini Terme, tel: 0572-77 22 44, fax: 70109.

San Miniato al Tedesco: APT, Piazza del Popolo 3, 56027 San Miniato, tel: 0571-42745, fax: 418739.

San Gimignano: APT, Piazza del Duomo 1, San Gimignano, tel: 0577-940008, fax: 940903.

Colle di Val d'Elsa: APT, Via Campana 18, 53034 Colle di Val d'Elsa, tel: 0577-922791, fax: 922621.

Volterra: APT, Via Giusto Turazza 2, 56048 Volterra, tel/fax: 0588-86150.

Livorno: APT, Piazza Cavour 6, 57100 Livorno, tel: 0586-898111, fax: 896173; Porto Mediceo, tel: 895320, and Stazione Marittima Calata Carrara, tel: 210331 (both 1 June–30 September).

Rosignano Marittimo: APT, Via Gramsci 7, Rosignano Marittimo, tel: 792973 (1 June–30 September).

Massa Marittima: Ufficio Turistica Alta Maremma Turismo (AMATUR), Via Norma Parenti 22, 58024 Massa Maritima, tel: 0566-902756, fax: 940095.

Montalcino: Ufficio Turistico Comunale, Costa del Municipio 8, 53024 Montalcino, tel/fax: 0577-849331.

Montepulciano: Ufficio Turistico Comunale, Via Ricci 9, 53045 Montepulciano, tel: 0578-757442.

Motorists

A national driving licence and country stickers suffice, though a green insurance card is recommended. Breakdown service is usually free of charge for members of automobile clubs.

Seat-belts are compulsory in Italy. Never leave anything in the car which might attract thieves – not even for a few moments. Also, remember that the fines for traffic offences in Italy (parking, overtaking, speed limits, etc) are incredibly high. On country roads the limit is usually 90kmph (55mph), and on motorways 130kmph (80mph); speed limits are often lowered at weekends or on public holidays.

Parking is expensive

Parking

Car parking in – and even vehicle access to – all the historic city centres is prohibited. The nearer you park to the centre of a city, the more expensive things get. All the larger towns and cities can be comfortably visited by rail (particularly cheap in Italy); cars are only really necessary for tours through the Tuscan landscape.

Money

The Italian currency is the lira (abbreviated to Lit. or L). Cheques may be exchanged up to a value of L400,000 at banks with the EC symbol. Most credit cards, including Visa, Access and American Express, are accepted in hotels, restaurants and shops and for air and train tickets and cash at any bank.

Shopping

This can be done everywhere. There are expensive fashion shops run by world-famous designers in Florence, stores selling elegant clothing and shoes in Lucca, and *objets d'art* on sale even in small towns. Tuscany is particularly famous for its leather, ceramic, marble and alabaster products. Bargains can often be discovered at weekly markets.

For further information, check the *Routes* section.

Tuscany is famous for its leather

Receipts

Not only the Italians themselves but also foreign tourists are expected to have receipts *(ricevuta fiscale)* made out by restaurants, hotels, car repair workshops, etc, listing services rendered plus the correct amount of Italian VAT (IVA) and to keep them on their person for possible checks by the Italian fiscal authorities. Failure to furnish receipts can often result in a stiff fine.

Tipping

This is expected, despite all-inclusive prices (approximately 10 percent).

Opening Times

Generally, *shops* are open on weekdays from 9am–7.30pm with a lunch break from 1–3.30pm. Many shops are closed on Saturday and Monday afternoons.

High standards of craftsmanship

Shops take long lunch breaks

Post your cards here

Banks: Monday to Friday 8.30am–1.30pm; some also open in the afternoon from 2.45pm–3.45pm. Money can be exchanged at weekends in the railway stations and airports of the larger cities. Money changing machines are also to be found at the main tourist centres.

Museum opening hours vary, and the times stated in this book are subject to change. State-owned museums are generally open from 9am–2pm, and 9am–1pm on Sunday and public holidays. They are often closed on Mondays. Note: some state-owned and municipal museums allow free admission to visitors under 18 and over 60 years of age.

Churches are usually closed around lunchtime, roughly from noon–4pm.

Filling Stations, apart from those on the motorways, are closed at lunchtime and on Sunday and public holidays. Some have cash-operated automatic pumps.

Public holidays

1 January (New Year); 6 January (Epiphany); Easter Monday; 1 May (Labour Day); 15 August (Assumption of the Virgin); 1 November (All Saints' Day); 8 December (the Immaculate Conception); 25/26 December (Christmas).

Postal services

Main post offices in major towns are open all day, otherwise the hours are 8am to 1.30pm. Stamps are sold at post offices and tobacconists. There are letter-boxes in most main streets, at post offices and railway stations.

Telephone

Calls can be made from phone centres run by the phone company Telecom. Coin-operated phones take L100, L200 and L500 coins and also *gettoni* (phone tokens), which can be purchased either over the counter or from special machines. A phone card *(scheda telefonica)* is a more convenient way of telephoning; these come in L5,000, L10,000 and 15,000 versions and are available from newspaper kiosks, tobacconists or from Telecom offices.

There is direct dialling to most countries. Within the country, use a three-number code which is different for each city. From abroad, dial 0039 then the area code number, dropping the inital 0. From Italy, dial the internatioanl code then the area code number, again dropping the initial 0. For information, dial 184.

AT&T: 172-1011, Sprint: 172-1877, MCI: 172-1022.

Time

Italy is six hours ahead of US Eastern Standard Time and one hour ahead of Greenwich Mean Time.

Voltage

Usually 220v; occasionally 110v. There are different plugs and sockets for each.

Medical

With Form E111 from the Department of Health and Social Security, UK visitors are entitled to reciprocal medical treatment in Italy. There are similar arrangements for other members of EU countries. It may nevertheless be advisable to take out insurance for private treatment in case of accident.

Holiday insurance policies and private patients schemes are recommended for non-EU visitors.

In case of minor ailments, chemists (*Farmacia*) are well stocked with medicines, often sold without prescription.

Emergencies

Emergency Assistance (Ambulance, fire, police), tel: 113.
Police Immediate Action, tel: 112.
Breakdown service, tel: 116.

Theft

Petty crime is a problem in Italy, particularly the snatching of handbags and jewellery. Always carry valuables securely either in a money belt or bag worn across the body. Report any thefts to the police, as evidence of the crime is required before an insurance claim can be made. Police Headquarters in Florence, Via Zara 2, tel: 055 49771.

Diplomatic representation

British Consulate: Palazzo Castelbarco, Lungarno Corsini 2, Florence, tel: 055-284133.
American Consulate: Lungarno Amerigo Vespucci 38, Florence, tel: 055-239 8276.

Italy is one hour ahead of GMT

Plush, modern luxury

Accommodation

There's a huge choice of accommodation possibilities in Tuscany, all tailored to individual preferences and pockets, ranging from Renaissance palazzos to country farmhouses. Hotels generally need to be booked well in advance in Florence and Siena. During local summer festivals, particularly the Sienese *Palio*, rooms are scarce.

Country houses, villas and apartments can all be organised via **The Best in Italy**, Via Ugo Foscolo 72, 50124 Florence, tel: 055-223064, fax: 055-229 8912.

Family holidays

There are attractive holiday villages *(Villaggi Turistici)* for families with children all over Tuscany, with bungalows, holiday houses, apartments and supermarkets (for addresses, contact any travel agent).

Get a feel for the country life

Farm stays

Farm stays *(Agriturismo)* are an excellent way of experiencing the Tuscan countryside while staying on a farm or a wine estate. One of the best guides to farm stays is *Vacanza e Natura, La Guida di Terranostra*, Terranostra, Via XXIV Maggio 43 Rome, tel: 06-468 2368/468 2370. Local tourist offices will also provide lists of possibilities. The regional *Agriturismo* booking centre is **Agriturist Ufficio Regionale**, Piazza di San Firenze 3, 50122 Florence, tel: 055-287838.

Hotels

Italian hotels are classified according to a 1–5 star rating system. For convenience, the following hotel suggestions are listed by town and accorded $$$ (expensive), $$ (moderate) or $ (inexpensive) price categories.

Arezzo (area code 0575)
$$Continentale, Piazza Guido Monaco 7, tel: 20251, fax: 350485; **$$Minerva**, Via Fiorentina 4, tel: 370390, fax: 302415; **$Cecco**, Corso Italia 215, tel: 20986, fax: 356730.

Colle di Val d'Elsa (area code 0577)
$$Arnolfo, Via Campana 8, tel: 922020, fax: 922324; **$$La Vecchia Cartiera,** Via Oberdan 5/9, tel: 921107, fax: 923688.

Cortona (area code 0575)
$$San Luca, Piazza Garibaldi 2, tel: 630460, fax: 630105; **$Athens**, Via S Antonio 12, tel: 630508, fax: 604457.

Fiesole (area code 055)
$$$Pensione Bencistà, Via Benedetto da Maiano 4, tel and fax: 59163.

Florence (area code 055)
$$$Torre di Bellosguardo, Via Roti Michelozzi 2, tel: 229 8145, fax: 229008; **$$$Loggiato dei Serviti**, Piazza SS Annunziata 3, tel: 289592, fax: 289595; **$$$Goldoni**, Via Borgo Ognissanti 8, tel: 284080, fax: 282576; **$$$Splendor**, Via S Gallo 30, tel: 483427, fax: 461276.

Livorno (area code 0586)
$$Hotel Touring, Via Goldoni 61, tel: 21080; **$$Palazzo**, Viale Italia 195, tel: 805371, fax: 803206.

Lucca (area code 0583)
$$$Villa La Principessa, Strada Statale del Brennero 1616, Massa Pisana, tel: 370037, fax: 379136; **$$Piccolo Hotel Puccini**, Via di Poggio, tel: 55421, fax: 53487; **$$La Luna**, Corte Compagni 12, tel: 493634, fax: 490021.

Many hotels have pools

Massa Marittima (area code 0566)
$$Il Sole, Via della Libertà 43, tel: 901971, fax: 901959; **$Duca del Mare**, Via D Alighieri 1/2, tel: 902284, fax: 901905; **$$Hotel Cris**, Via Roma 9/10, Anglo Via Cappellini, tel: 903830.

Montepulciano (area code 0578)
$$Granducato, Via delle Lettere 62, tel/fax: 758610; **$$Il Borghetto**, Borgo Buio 7, tel/fax: 757354.

Montalcino (area code 0577)
$$Il Giglio, Via Soccorso Saloni 5, tel: 848167; **$Il Giardino**, Via Cavour 4, tel: 848257.

Pescia (area code 0573)
$$Azienda Agricola Marzalla, Via Collechio 1, tel: 47010.

Most have flower displays

Royal Victoria, Pisa

Pienza (area code 0578)
$$Corsignano, Via della Madonnina 11, tel: 748501, fax: 748166.

Pisa (area code 050)
$$$Grand Hotel Duomo, Via S Maria 94, tel: 561894, fax: 560418; **$$Royal Victoria**, Lungarno Pacinotti 12, tel: 940111, fax: 940180; **$$Verdi**, Piazza della Republica 5, tel/fax: 598947; **$Di Stefano**, Via Sant'Apollonia 35, tel/fax: 553559.

Pistoia (area code 0573)
$$Leon Bianco, Via Panciatichi 2, tel: 26675, fax: 26704; **$$Il Convento**, Via S Quirico 33, 51030 Santomato, tel: 453578, fax: 452651. **$$Firenze**, Via Curtatatone e Montanara 42, tel: 23141.

Prato (area code 0574)
$$$Villa S Cristina, Via Poggio Secco 58, tel: 595951, fax: 57623; **$$–$$$Flora**, Via Cairoli 31, tel: 33521, fax: 40289.

San Gimignano (area code 0577)
$$Leon Bianco, Piazza della Cisterna 13, tel: 941294, fax: 942123; **$$La Cisterna**, Piazza della Cisterna 24, tel: 940328, fax: 942080.

San Miniato al Tedesco (area code 0571)
$$Albergo Miravalle, Piazza Castello 3, tel: 418075, fax: 419681.

Hotel Certosa di Maggiano

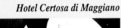

Siena (area code 0577)
$$$Hotel Certosa di Maggiano, Via Certosa 82, tel: 288180, fax: 288189; **$$Palazzo Ravizza**, Pian dei Mantellini 34, tel: 280462, fax: 271370; **$$Chiusarelli**, Via Curtatone 15, tel: 280562, fax: 271177; **$Garibaldi**, Via Duprè 18, tel: 284204.

Volterra (area code 0588)
$$–$$$Hotel San Lino, Via San Lino 26, tel: 85250, fax: 80620; **$$Hotel Etruria**, Via Matteotti 32, tel/fax: 87377.

Some cities have organisations specialising in hotel reservations:

Florence: **Consorzio Informazioni Turistiche Alberghiere** (in the main station), tel: 282893; at the motorway service areas of Peretola Sud and Chianti Est, and also in the Fortezza da Basso (1 April–10 September).
Siena: **Siena Hotels Promotion**, Piazza San Domenico, tel: 288084, fax: 280290.

Campsites

Tuscany has numerous campsites and most are well-equipped, especially those along the Tyrrhenian Sea; in summer (July and August) it's best to reserve in advance. This is a selection of addresses; comprehensive lists of campsites are available from ENIT offices or from the Federazione Italiana del Campeggio, Via Vittorio Emanuele 11, 50041 Calenzano.

Florence: **Viale Michelangelo** (1 April–31 October), below the Piazzale Michelangelo; **Villa Camerata**, Viale A Righi 2–4, on hillside facing Fiesole.

Fiesole: In the **Prato e Pini** suburb, high above Florence and pleasantly cool.

Pisa: **'Torre Pendente'**, Viale delle Cascine 86, 1km (½ mile) outside the city, open 15 March to 15 October.

Montecatini Terme, open all year, 3km (1 ¾ miles) **north** of town, with pool (April to October).

San Gimignano: in **Santa Lucia**, 1km (½ mile) out of town, small site, April–mid-October.

Volterra: **'Le Balze'**, 1km (½ mile) out of town, pleasant, plenty of shade.

Livorno: At **Antignano** by the sea (May to September) and Montenero in the hills.

Youth Hostels

These are located in Tuscany at Abetone, Arezzo, Cortona, Florence, Greve in Chianti, Lucca, Marina di Massa, Montaione, Pisa, San Gimignano, Siena, Tavarnelle Val di Pesa and Volterra. For more information contact the **Associazione Italiana Alberghi per la Gioventù**, Via Cavour 44, 00184 Roma, tel: 06-487 1152, fax: 4880492.

Reserve your pitch in advance

Index